The Real Miracle

Harley Dickson

PROVIDENCE HOUSE PUBLISHERS
Franklin, Tennessee

Copyright 2000 by Providence United Methodist Church

All rights reserved. Written permission must be secured from the publisher to use or reproduce any part of this book, except for brief quotations in critical reviews or articles.

Printed in the United States of America

04   03   02   01   00   1   2   3   4   5

Library of Congress Catalog Card Number: 99-69305

ISBN: 1-57736-176-8

Cover design by Gary Bozeman

PROVIDENCE HOUSE PUBLISHERS
238 Seaboard Lane • Franklin, Tennessee 37067
800-321-5692
www.providencehouse.com

I do not know his name,
But yet
I know he passed this way,
Because I was revived
Beside a well he dug
That I might drink
And gain some fresh, new strength.

I do not know his creed
Or color,
I only know that,
Weary, fainting, I have found
Sweet rest beneath the friendly shade
Of trees he planted as he passed
Through Baca's vale.

Aye, blessed, blessed is the man
Who, passing through
The valley
Digs a well.

—Author Unknown

Alice and Bill White

WITHOUT RESERVE THIS STORY IS DEDICATED TO BILL AND ALICE WHITE, FOR WITHOUT them there would be no Haiti Mission of Providence United Methodist Church in Charlotte, North Carolina. And, without the inspiration of their commitment, hundreds of us would have missed the joy of participating in this mission.

CONTENTS

PREFACE	xi
ACKNOWLEDGMENTS	xiii
INTRODUCTION A Village Called Tovar	3
CHAPTER 1 The Boat	8
CHAPTER 2 A Journey of Faith	12
CHAPTER 3 A Growing Involvement	17
CHAPTER 4 The "Look-See Mission"	24
CHAPTER 5 The First Steps	29
CHAPTER 6 A Time to Prepare	38

CHAPTER 7 The Trailblazers	44
CHAPTER 8 The Builders	51
CHAPTER 9 The Doctors	60
CHAPTER 10 The Surgeons	74
CHAPTER 11 The Real Miracle	82
CHAPTER 12 Does It Matter?	86
APPENDICES	93
APPENDIX A Chronology—Haiti Mission	95
APPENDIX B Haiti Mission Directory (List of Participants)	103
APPENDIX C Maps of Haiti	107
INDEX	111

Preface

NOT LONG AFTER REV. GEORGE THOMPSON WAS APPOINTED SENIOR PASTOR OF PROVIDENCE UNITED METHODIST CHURCH, Alice and Bill White invited a group of Haiti Mission "vets" to their home for a reunion gathering. The purpose—to meet George and to share with him information about the mission.

It was a time for remembering; it was an inspiring evening. Stories were told, experiences shared, and life-changing events relived. Gradually two things became apparent. First, the wonderful story of the Haiti Mission was well worth telling and retelling; and second, except for the Whites, none of us knew the whole story.

As a group, we reflected on the oft-told tale of the blind men describing an elephant. Each described what he touched or felt, but none could picture the entire animal. Some, like me, were well versed in the beginning of the Haiti Mission but had little firsthand knowledge of subsequent events. There were also many faithful participants who knew little or nothing about its fascinating origin.

During the evening someone raised a question. "Wouldn't it be great if we had a way to share this story with more people?" With even the Whites having selective memories from their twenty-year involvement, shouldn't the story be put in writing in order to preserve it? On the way home that evening Inez, in a manner befitting only a wife, put it to me this way, "You are the one who ought to do it!"

Knowing I had no good reason not to do it, she reopened the conversation on several occasions. Finally, her persistence and my personal interest combined to bring about a decision: "Why not?" So it was in this way, and without serious opposition, that I became the designated storyteller.

xi

Months later, after many conversations with participants, exposure to a multitude of files and photos, and another informative visit to Haiti, I am fully convinced that this story is not only worth preserving but needs to be shared with a much wider audience.

I am further convinced that this is not my story. Rather, it is a continuing saga of God's involvement with one family, one church, and a host of others who possess a deep and meaningful commitment. These concrete examples of Christian mission call attention to volunteers who have made a real difference in a place of overwhelming need.

Should the telling of this story inspire even one more person to become personally involved in missions, it is worth the effort.

Acknowledgments

THE REAL MIRACLE RELATES THE EXPLOITS OF A LARGE NUMBER OF PEOPLE WITHOUT WHOM THERE WOULD BE NO Haiti Mission. I am indebted to many of these who took time to sit with me and share their memories, especially Alice and Bill White, Bill James, Dick and Louise Maybin, Mike Barringer, Mary Coleman, Al Rose, Howard Boylan, Larry Wilkinson, and George Freeman.

These personal memories would not have been sufficient without the extensive records, reports, lists, diaries, and logs kept independently by Alice and Bill. They provided the factual information that served to keep me on track. I am especially grateful to Bill White who arranged a guided tour for me in January of this year. Seeing all the Haiti work sites firsthand gave me a window through which I could visualize the events contained in the Haiti files. Photographs and slides came from the collections of participants too numerous to name individually.

It was the Publications Committee who gave many hours of their time proofreading, editing, and otherwise providing wise counsel during the preparation of the book. This group consisted of Al Rose, Mary Coleman, Inez Dickson, George Thompson, Howard and Carolyn Boylan, and Alice and Bill White. They guided the entire process. Their help was invaluable.

To all who participated in this mission, personally, financially, or otherwise, I offer profound appreciation. If your part of the story is not contained in this writing, the fault is mine. There was simply no way to include everything. But I do know that without each of you there would be no Haiti Mission. Thank you for all you have done and continue to do. You are the *real miracle*.

Finally, of utmost importance is the support of the membership of Providence United Methodist Church. You provided financially through the church budget and with your individual contributions. Even more importantly, you provided an institutional base for this mission. You opened a door through which members and participants from across the Southeast and beyond found their way to involvement in Christian mission. We thank you for your support. You are indeed a living legend on the community grapevine.

The Real Miracle

Introduction

A Village Called Tovar

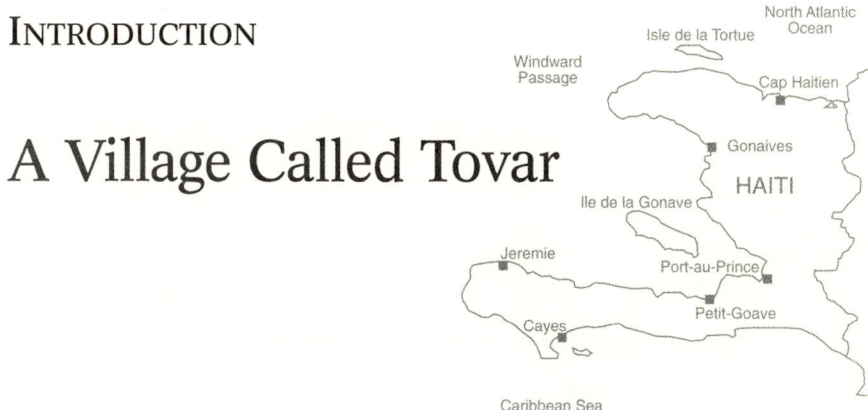

ONCE UPON A TIME, IN THE NORTHERN RURAL REGION OF THE LAND CALLED HAITI, THERE WAS A VILLAGE—ITS NAME was Tovar. While not a place from long, long ago, it is far away. So it takes a great deal of imagination to picture this village that provides the setting for our story.

Imagine first that you had been born in a city of 25,000 persons and lived in the same place all of your life. Now further imagine what it would have been like if there had been no doctor, no nurse, nor any clinically trained medical professional, to help you with those childhood diseases or other illnesses. And what if there had been no hospital or clinic to help you deal with accidents or emergencies? Suppose, also, that you had lived without clean drinking water or indoor plumbing. And, of course, without electricity there would have been no telephone, radio, or television.

Then contemplate living under those conditions, not in a city, but in a rugged rural mountainous setting. In a village of mud and stick huts with thatched roofs and dirt floors, there existed only the slimmest possibility that you could grow enough food to keep your family alive. Only with this kind of imagination can you begin to sense what it was like to live in Tovar as few as fifteen years ago.

When a group from Providence United Methodist Church in Charlotte, North Carolina, came to visit in 1982, this is exactly what they found. Struggling against the worst of odds, the people were eking out a bare existence. Poverty, malnutrition, disease, and starvation were everywhere. Conditions were appalling.

A typical thatched roof and woven stick "home" in 1982.

While statistics tell us that Haiti is the poorest nation in the Western Hemisphere, no secondhand information offers a realistic introduction to this third world country. Mary Coleman later described it this way:

> Nothing prepared me for the impact of my first visit. The sights, the sounds, the smells, the crowds . . . created an almost overwhelming effect when I first arrived. Like most Americans, I had never experienced the kind of abject poverty and lack of creature comforts most Haitians experience lifelong.

Dr. Bill James, a dentist on many of the medical teams, described his feelings: "I was surprised by the poverty. Many people have no homes and simply wander around. The local garbage dump is a busy place, where Haitians (those few who can afford it) pay to get in just to find some food for the day."

The Providence group had come to find people they could help—a place where folks from their church could have a hands-on involvement in missions. Certainly, those here were far less fortunate, with a huge variety of needs. It was a place where people really could use what the group had to give. But quickly, they discovered something else as well. The people of Haiti had a lot to give them in return. As one member observed, "Haiti has an economic poverty that defies description, yet the

A Village Called Tovar

people have not lost their hope or their basic concern for their fellow man. There is no poverty of spirit."

Coming at the invitation of the Haitian Methodist Church, they found a group of Christians who read the same Bible, sang the same songs, and observed the same rituals. Their language was Creole, but in worship a common bond was shared. In a later visit the Reverend George Freeman expressed a feeling shared by most that have been there: "We are different, but in our worship experience we are one. Each of us has the possibility for new life in the one who came not to be served, but to serve."

The quiet simplicity of the faith of Haitian Christians was inspiring. Those who came to Haiti to help found help and healing for themselves. While the people looked different, spoke a different language, and lived under appalling conditions, there was a common tie. To hold hands with your brothers and sisters and sing, each in one's own language, "Blest Be the Tie That Binds" is a moving experience. No longer are these people strangers or statistics from the pages of a book. They are real human beings, your Christian friends.

It was in this part of Haiti that a relationship was formed and a commitment born. The group returned home with a resolve to come back and do what they could to help—to make the resources of their church available to these new friends, in whatever way they could. As Alice

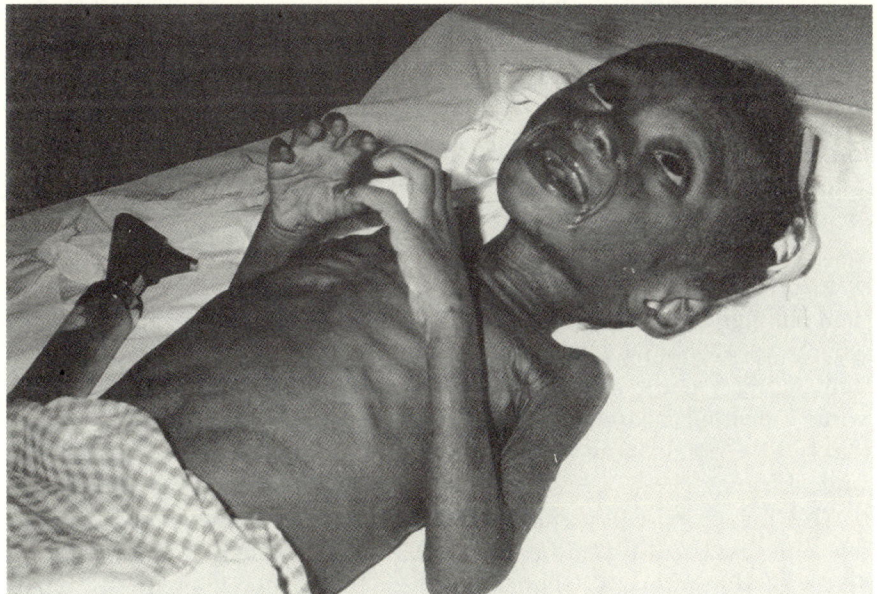

Children are most affected by malnutrition and disease.

White said, "Though you come home weary and saddened, at the end you say, *how can I not go back?*"

And every year, since 1982, members of Providence United Methodist Church have been back. Time after time they returned and took others with them, more than 150 in all—from many churches and more than a dozen states and Puerto Rico. Working together with the Haitian Methodist Church and the Haitian Ministry of Health, they dug wells, helped build clinics and churches, and sent two or three medical teams each year. The doctors went at their own expense and treated whatever patients they could while they were there. Much medicine and medical supplies were donated and brought or shipped to Haiti. Teams of surgeons also volunteered to work in two of the Christian hospitals in the larger towns of Cap Haitien and Limbé.

Successes, even small ones, are celebrated, and it was rewarding when as many as twelve hundred patients received help during a week's time. However, frustrations often loomed larger than successes. Clinics that had been built stood vacant for months until another medical team returned. It was disheartening to know of those Haitians who desperately needed help but who had not received it. They had waited patiently, but when time ran out and the team had to leave, no one was there to help until months later when the next team arrived. Nor had there been any follow-up treatment for the patients who had already been seen.

From the beginning, it was the long-term goal for this mission to support the establishment and operation of permanent, year-round clinics at Tovar, Latannerie, and Dondon. Finally, after long years of frustration, the first part of that dream was realized.

In December of 1997, the Tovar Clinic, about an hour's drive from the northern coastal city of Cap Haitien, opened as a full-time, fully staffed community health center. There was no fanfare except for a prayer before an audience of sick people waiting for help. But the efforts of the first year certainly provided cause for celebration. During that twelvemonth period, over 6,275 persons received medical care, approximately 45 percent of them children. Also, it was possible to transfer quite a few critical surgical patients to Hopital Le Bon Samaritain (Hospital Good Samaritan) in Limbé, forty-five minutes away. It is there that Dr. Mike Barringer (Shelby, North Carolina), also a part of the Haiti Mission of Providence United Methodist Church, now spends three months out of each year with a surgical team.

The Tovar Clinic, a combined effort of the Development Program of Eglisé Methodiste d'Haiti (the Haitian Methodist Church), the Ministry of Health of Haiti, and the Haiti Mission of Providence United Methodist Church, is a dream come true. Now, each year in January, May, and

October, teams averaging ten in number work side by side with the permanent staff seeing and treating patients. In addition, their doctors and nurses have the opportunity to learn more about American medicine, while our people learn certain essentials of the Haitian culture. Providence groups now take a great deal of satisfaction in knowing that when they return home, patients will be cared for on a year-round basis.

With the opening of the Tovar Clinic comes a realistic hope that a second permanent clinic can be staffed at Latannerie, another remote Haitian village. But in the face of such overwhelming need, even this seems insignificant. Disease and poverty still abound. Sometimes the situation seems totally hopeless. What is one clinic, or even two or three, in the midst of the appalling health conditions that still exist?

But think again! Suppose Tovar was *your town*? What if you had lived there all your life, without any hope for help? Even the most basic health care would be nothing short of a miracle.

It is the story of this village, this place, and this region, which I share with you. It is a narrative relating how the personal interests of Bill and Alice White became entwined with the desire of Providence United Methodist Church to become involved in mission work. It is a continuing saga involving Providence members, and many others from over a dozen states, who are a part of a mission of outreach to the poor in Haiti—now their friends.

In the face of innumerable obstacles and overwhelming odds, this story, spanning two decades, is a tale of many miracles. But sharing the real miracle must wait for the rest of the story to unfold.

CHAPTER 1

The Boat

THE VERY BEGINNING OF THE STORY IS SOMEWHAT UNUSUAL. IT BEGAN WITH A GIFT. THERE MAY SEEM TO BE NOTHING especially unusual about that; gifts are made all the time. But what happened can be deemed extraordinary, if not miraculous.

The gift was a bit out of the ordinary in that it was not cash, nor a check, nor even stocks or bonds. It was a gift of personal property. The gift was a boat belonging to Bill White. The *Pieces of Eight*, as the boat was named, had been in the White family for ten years. The fifty-foot motor-sailer with twin diesel engines was the only sailboat on the East Coast fitted with outriggers for marlin fishing. This, along with its capacity to be at home on the ocean for days at a time, allowed the Whites and their friends happily to enjoy sailing, fishing, and vacationing in and out of the Chesapeake Bay and down the Atlantic coast as far as Miami. Also, Bill frequently used the boat to entertain customers, clients, and business associates.

Fun times were interspersed with scary ones. Once a Russian trawler attempted to ram the vessel because White's fishing party accidentally cut the trawler's "long" lines. On another occasion, the U.S. Navy cruiser SS *Manley Rodgers* mistakenly shelled it, and once in darkest night it almost sailed into an aircraft carrier. Several times the *Pieces of Eight* wallowed safely through sudden storms that frequent the Atlantic. Ten years of pleasant memories still linger for those who shared these experiences.

But nothing prepared the White family for Bill's surprise announcement at their family gathering on Christmas Eve 1979, "I'm going to give the boat to the church!"

The response was both vocal and pretty much unanimous. Almost with one voice the family responded, "You can't give *our boat* away."

However, Bill's determination proved stronger than any protests or questions. Like all boats, it was expensive to maintain and operate, and in fact, the family had not used it very much in quite a while. For these reasons, Bill started looking for the best way to dispose of the boat and replace it with a family cottage at the beach.

Then, as now, boats are frequently bought and sold, but negotiations can be lengthy and the price unpredictable. The U.S. tax laws in 1980 provided an alternative sometimes used—donating the boat to charity. Selling the boat would trigger a substantial tax liability, while a donation might more than offset that with a charitable deduction. As Bill explored his options, a donation (provided a willing recipient could be found) began to make good financial sense. It was with this in mind that Bill proceeded to announce, "I'm giving the boat to the church!"

Why the church? His decision was well grounded in his Methodist upbringing and his continuing interest in that denomination's work. His father, A. R. White Sr., had headed the regional office of the Methodist Publishing House first in Dallas, Texas, then Nashville, Tennessee, and later in Richmond, Virginia. He rendered distinguished service to the Methodist Church as a lifetime employee of the publishing house and is often credited for the inspiration behind changing its official name to the current name, "Cokesbury." As might be expected, when Bill and his family moved to Charlotte, they followed their heritage, remained Methodists, and became members of Providence United Methodist Church.

Earlier, one of their four children, daughter Alicia, married Dick Daily, a United Methodist minister. (One more reason for considering the church as the beneficiary of the gift.) In 1979 Dick was the associate minister at Morrison Church in Leesburg, Florida. Prior to the Christmas Eve announcement, it was only with him that Bill had discussed the possible gift. "If I give the boat do you think the church would accept it?" It was Dick's ventured opinion that it could and would.

Thus the surprise Christmas Eve announcement. Alice White later remarked, "I was shocked when he bought it when we were in Miami ten years ago, and I was shocked when he announced he was giving it away." Later she described other feelings as well, "It's a little sad. The boat has given us a lot of happy times and other memories which weren't exactly fun at the time."

Events remained in somewhat suspended animation following Christmas. The subject was dropped; seemingly no one wanted to discuss it further. And then on Super Bowl Sunday the first of the many miracles associated with the *Pieces of Eight* occurred. Bill and Alice went to Leesburg for a visit with Dick and Alicia. By happenstance, or providentially, whichever you choose to call it, Vera and Tommy Fadley also were visiting the Dailys on that January weekend. Friends from seminary days at Duke University Divinity School, they were serving as missionaries with the United Methodist Committee on Relief (UMCOR). Returning from Africa, and on their way to the home office in New York City, they *just happened* to stop by to see Dick and Alicia. It also *just happened* that their mission sponsor was Highland Park United Methodist Church in Dallas, Texas—Bill White's former church located three miles from his boyhood home.

Of course, it *just happened* that a discussion of the Christmas Eve event ensued. So confident were the Fadleys that the announced gift could be used, that they boldly accepted the boat on behalf of UMCOR.

Having been given pictures of the boat, the Fadleys hand-delivered these to the New York office upon their return. It was only three days later that Dr. Harry Haines, executive director of UMCOR, telephoned Bill in Charlotte and formally accepted the gift—with one stipulation, "Can you deliver the boat?" Without knowing where, Bill replied, "I guess I can, where do you want it?" And Dr. Haines answered, "In Port-au-Prince." To which Bill responded, "Where in the world is that?"

Little did he know what lay in store for him in this place he knew nothing about. Nor did he suspect the ways this journey would consume his interest and change his life, as well as the lives of hundreds of others. What began as a tax-wise transaction was being transformed into a spiritual odyssey. Did all of this *just happen*—or was it providential? You decide.

Without knowing or realizing the full impact of his decision, Bill had agreed to move the *Pieces of Eight* from its mooring in Lynnhaven Inlet in Virginia Beach, Virginia, to Port-au-Prince, capital of the nation of Haiti. At an average of six knots, the sixteen-hundred-mile journey would be an arduous and time-consuming trip, across the open waters of the Atlantic, through the Bahamas, and again across the Gulfstream to Hispanola. So to friends and family went out a cry for help. "Help me fix up the boat for the journey, and help me sail it to Haiti."

Thus, six months of preparation began for what would be a six-week journey. With some promises of financial aid, but mostly out of Bill's own resources, the gargantuan task got under way. Holding a full-time job meant that almost every minute of every weekend and all available vacation time had to be devoted to this project, and it was. Over three hundred hours were spent working in the oily, greasy, smelly, and often unbearably hot engine room of the *Pieces of Eight*.

From February through July of 1980 this became a priority. Each of the two diesel engines got a thorough overhaul, every hose and clamp was replaced, and all potential trouble spots checked and repaired, if necessary. Following a precedent not unlike that of Noah's ark, two spares for every part were stockpiled on the boat—two injectors, two batteries, and right down the line. Every conceivable emergency that might occur on the trip, or later in Haiti, was anticipated. So thorough was the preparation that amazingly nothing malfunctioned on the voyage except the refrigerator. The boat sailed four years in Haiti, and no additional parts were needed except those already stored on board.

All that remained was to get supplies aboard, chart a course, and obtain necessary permits. The trip was to be made in four stages and crew members readily volunteered. Immediate family members—with the exception of daughter Ginny who was preparing to enter college—and several friends agreed to accompany Bill on some part of the trip. R. M. White Sr. and R. M. White Jr. (brother and nephew), and E. H. Williamson, an engineer friend from Columbia, South Carolina, also signed on.

Son Paul White and Colonel and Mrs. William Love were to be on board on the first leg to Morehead City where Paul would come ashore and Alice White would join the crew along with John Burmeister. At Freeport they would disembark, and Dick and Alicia Daily would join Bill and continue through the Bahamas and on to the Exumas. There, son Rob and his wife Kathy, Hank and Elizabeth Lacy, Bill's dear friend Ray Scrivener, and Dr. Harry Haines, representing UMCOR, would replace them for the final leg.

The *Pieces of Eight* was ready. It was time for the historic journey to begin.

Chapter 2

A Journey of Faith

THE UPCOMING JOURNEY ATTRACTED ATTENTION FROM A WIDE AUDIENCE. KAYS GARY, NOTED FEATURE WRITER FOR THE *Charlotte Observer*, devoted a full column to it on August 5, 1980. Entitling the story "Pleasure Ship to Sail for God" he began: "The hurricane season has begun, Caribbean waters are full of drug-running pirates, and he'll be skirting the north shore of restless Cuba, but A. R. White Jr. is about to sail his fifty-foot boat to Haiti. The three week voyage doesn't intimidate him."

Bill's single-minded focus on preparation left little room for fear, but others were dubious about the safety of the boat and crew. In 1980 navigation for a sixteen-hundred-mile ocean voyage was less than precise. With little predictable radio contact and nothing more than obsolete Loran fixes to guide the boat, following an exact course was not easy. To make matters worse, five hurricanes had been spotted in the Atlantic, one of which (Alan) hit the Haiti coast while the *Pieces of Eight* was at sea. The greatest danger was the saturation of the Bahamian waters with drug runners, regularly hijacking small boats and converting them to their illicit purposes. The Coast Guard strongly advised against a boat sailing alone in these waters.

During an interview Alice White acknowledged, "There is considerable excitement about the delivery of the gift boat." Then she added, "With us there are mixed feelings. Mainly we want a safe trip for Bill."

Friends were naturally concerned, but one friend and former missionary put the journey in its spiritual perspective by saying, "His main protection will be that of all Christians. He has made an expensive commitment, with practically no assistance. Bill White will be all right."

Bill White at the helm of the Pieces of Eight *on its 1980 voyage.*

On the strength of that kind of faith the journey began. It is best described in these words from the ship's log:

> It reminded me of someone saying goodbye. She edged along the pier, paused for a moment and then moved away. It was the last time the boat would lie at this dock. She moved out of Long Creek at 1900 EDT on August 8, 1980, into Broad Bay, through Lynnhaven Inlet and the Chesapeake Bay, passed Cape Henry Lighthouse and headed south on her final voyage as our boat. Her destination was Port-au-Prince, Haiti.

Excerpts from the ship's log, supplemented by Alice's notes, tell about the rest of the trip.

> On August 8, 1980, a boat called the "Pieces of Eight" sailed out into the Atlantic, and unbeknownst to anyone then, she launched a mission as well.
>
> Boatmen in South Florida urged the owners not to make the voyage through the islands. "If they want the boat let them come and get it." During those years, particularly in 1979 and 1980, there had been several incidents of pirating of small sailing vessels in the Bahamas. Those on

board, either owners or charters, were murdered and thrown overboard, and their boats taken to be used for transport of drugs. Tourists began cruising in groups, and it was not uncommon to see a fleet of Morgan Out-islanders, Nauticats, and Columbias cruising in close formation. The solitary "Pieces of Eight" slowly making her way through Bahamian waters was an unusual sight.

One night, sometime between 10 P.M. and 2 A.M., after leaving Nassau Harbor, there was a faint light aft of us, which followed our course, and it appeared to get stronger and closer. Gaetane Cato and I were standing watch, and during the time we observed the light, we agreed that it had to be a boat faster than ours. When the Captain came up on deck to check our course, we reported our observations, and he too saw the light, which by now was clearly larger and brighter. In the darkness he couldn't see the size of our eyes.

While the captain said that he was certain that there was no danger, he turned off all lights aboard, and we ran the remainder of the night in darkness. Sometime after that, the light behind us disappeared, either because our stalker turned off his lights or changed course. For the rest of our watch we looked over our shoulder much more frequently than we checked forward. We laughed about the possibility of running into something broadside while we were straining to see something behind us in the dark.

There were many who wanted to take part in this expedition, and so there were crew changes in Morehead City, Freeport, and Georgetown, Exuma, where certain members of the crew flew in and others flew home. For each one leaving, there was a heave and a sigh, and one long backward glance at the boat they would never see again. After Georgetown, there were no more ports before Port-au-Prince.

Then a strange thing happened. I got four definite Loran fixes, only one of which had come in clearly prior to that, and I could tell that I was twenty-six miles off of Haiti. The visibility was very good, the seas four to six, and the wind was running out of the southeast. It was about midnight.

Ray—one of the crew—yelled, "I see something strange. It looks like the mountains of Haiti." We walked aft, and looked out over the Bimini top and past the sail, and there low-lying in the mist by the light of the full moon were the mountains of Haiti, and the ocean, and the boat, and the lives of six people, and the responsibility temporarily bore upon me.

A Journey of Faith

About fifteen miles off Haiti, I set a course for the Southwest, which put the wind at our backs, and immediately it was calm. The boat was going down the sea. All this time, for the last nine months, I had the feeling that I was being told what to do. This was the first time that the wind had not been on our bow, for the first time I was not fighting the sea. There's something about Haiti. There is something there.

On August 25, 1980, the "Pieces of Eight" motored into the harbor at Port-au-Prince with Dr. Harry Haines at the helm. She was not met by cheering crowds, but by a shallow ship's channel with sticks for markers leaning this way and that, and she went aground briefly.

On the dock there was a little man with a friendly face and a funny straw hat. His name was Guido, and appropriately to his name, he offered to guide the Captain to the customs dock in his rowboat. And thanks to Guido, the boat did not go aground again.

While the crew remained aboard, the Captain searched Port-au-Prince for the Customs Officer, with the help of another friendly Haitian doctor with a very old car. It was late at night when the papers were signed, and the boat properly dealt with.

On the third day, many officials and their wives and children from Eglisé Methodiste d'Haiti came down to see the boat and to greet those aboard. Also present was the head of the Methodist Church in the Caribbean. Probably about forty people boarded the boat for the welcoming ceremony, to the consternation of the Captain. He hated the thought that she might sink so soon after her arrival.

A good day was had by all, with Haitian Methodists excited about new possibilities open to them now that the *Pieces of Eight* was safely in port. Personnel and supplies could be transported to the island of La Gonave where 20,000 persons lived with little connection to the main part of Haiti. Jeremie, and several towns on the far western shore of the main island, could easily be reached by boat as well.

The mission was accomplished! The journey had been completed with great effort, at significant cost, but miraculously without incident. Even with the primitive navigation systems on board, the boat was never off course. With five hurricanes churning through the same waters during its sixteen-hundred-mile voyage, not a drop of rain touched the deck of the *Pieces of Eight*. Only the refrigerator broke down and that was easily repaired. In every other way the boat ran

16 THE REAL MIRACLE

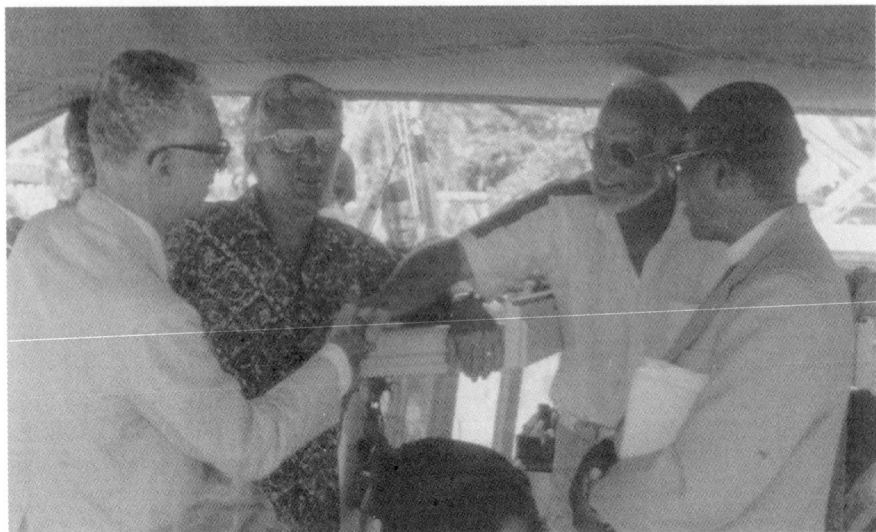

Bill White and Dr. Harry Haines officially turn over the Pieces of Eight *to Rev. Edouard Domond, the general superintendent of the Eglisé Methodiste and a representative of MCCA.*

perfectly. No accident marred the safety of the crew members.

Bill White could now breathe a big sigh of relief and rejoice in the successful conclusion of an effort now behind him. Or so it seemed.

But something had happened during those eight months. Both Bill and Alice developed a strong attachment to this strange country. On first sighting land Bill had remarked in the captain's log, "There's something about Haiti. There is something there." With every subsequent experience new feelings emerged. "We were profoundly touched by all we saw and learned through this experience," wrote Alice. "I think both of us felt there must be some other ways we could help."

Please follow as the miracle story of the boat continues and then plays out to its conclusion. But prepare yourself for the emergence of another story. It involves a deepening commitment of the Whites, and the way their love for Haiti inspired the involvement of Providence United Methodist Church.

Chapter 3

A Growing Involvement

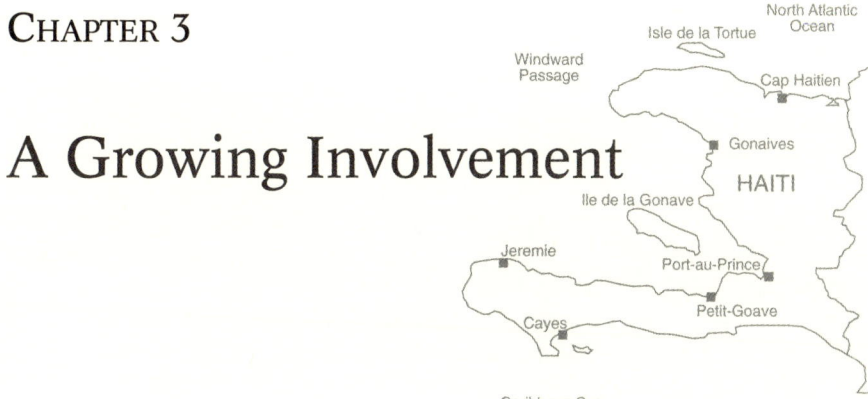

UP TO THIS POINT, THE INVOLVEMENT IN HAITI WAS ALMOST EXCLUSIVELY BILL'S. BY ALICE'S ADMISSION IT WAS *HIS THING*. Out of respect for his strong determination, she chose to support what he was doing. However, it was not long before circumstances began to happen that involved the two of them.

Following the delivery of the boat in August of 1980, the next visit to Haiti was in late December. Sometimes referred to as the Christmas trip, it was Alice's first time in Haiti. The occasion was a meeting of the Board of Directors of UMCOR, to which the Whites were invited, and where their gift was acknowledged. Several events on this trip played a pivotal role in shaping their future involvement in Haiti.

Alice had flown with Bill to Port-au-Prince in their single engine six-passenger Cherokee airplane. When introduced to Bishop Wayne K. Clymer, president of UMCOR, Alice referred to herself as "just the airplane driver's wife." This was not to be the case for very long. Later describing her feelings about the trip, she said, "We were profoundly touched by all we saw and learned through this experience." And, as is often the case with persons exposed to the extreme conditions of poverty in Haiti, she began to ask, "What can I do to help?"

As a professional engineer with credentials and experience in water purification, waste treatment, and construction, there was little doubt Bill could make a contribution. But what was Alice qualified to do? She was the mother of four children, now grown, and a college graduate with majors in art and psychology. On their farm she had bred, raised, and trained horses; and a host of people, especially children and youth, had been trained in the finer arts of horsemanship under her tutelage.

But to her, it did not seem that any of this background could be very useful in Haiti.

However, during this trip, one facet of Haitian life did capture her attention. Continually, she was overwhelmed by the poor health of the people and by their inability to cope with disease and malnutrition. It was also during this visit that Alice met Alberto Dussex. In August, her son Rob had struck up a chance conversation with this man who was a worker at the Royal Haitian Hotel just across the street from the dock where the *Pieces of Eight* was moored. Severely crippled in an auto accident as a youth, Alberto walked and worked with great difficulty. Rob suggested to his mother that she might want to meet him. And she did.

Venturing out on her own, through the iron gates of the dock area and onto the streets crowded with people who spoke only Creole, was a scary thing. But Alice, anything but timid, made her way to the Royal Haitian and asked for Alberto. And there he was. All that Rob had told his mother was true, and more. He did work at the hotel and for a very special reason. Before Alberto was employed, the manager had lost a large amount of cash while walking to the bank. Knowing it was surely gone forever, he was more than surprised when Alberto showed up at the hotel to return the money he had found on the street. So unusual was that kind of honesty that the manager hired him on the spot, and he had been a trusted employee ever since.

Alice was deeply moved by Alberto's physical condition and his honesty, and she and Bill spent the better part of a year arranging a visa and passport so he could come to Charlotte for medical examination and therapy. Several doctors were willing to provide their services without charge. But it was the Whites who kept Alberto, as a guest in their home, for five months until he was able to return to Haiti.

While Alice now says this event was not crucial in determining her later decisions, it was certainly a strong indication of the way poverty and need in Haiti moved her to want to help. And, in fact, immediately upon returning from the Christmas trip, she signed up for several nursing classes at the Central Piedmont Community College in Charlotte.

"In the beginning I had no intention of getting a degree," she said. "That was more than I had in mind." However, with a growing commitment to Haiti, her resolve increased, and in the spring quarter she enrolled in the clinical nursing program. Already having a bachelor of arts degree, she chose the associate program, and in 1984 she received her associate degree in Nursing. Shortly thereafter, she passed the North Carolina Licensing Board examinations and became certified as a registered nurse. Later describing the commitment that carried her through these years she said:

I felt very certain that while it was my decision to become a nurse, that there was a force—which had to be greater than I, that moved me in that direction, and helped me throughout. It was the most difficult task I had ever undertaken—but there was such a need in Haiti—and I was healthy, physically and mentally, with many good years in which to give something of myself—for the first time in my life.

Meanwhile, Bill became involved in a different way. Quickly it became apparent that the Haitians needed more training for the *Pieces of Eight* to be useful to them. For example, the boat could not always be started because the batteries had not been sufficiently charged. This happened because no one was adding battery acid. They needed more instruction.

Fortunately, on the Christmas trip Bill met Benny Neal, a person who could help. A Kentucky native with a mechanical background and construction experience, Benny had just come to Haiti to work with UMCOR and the United Methodist Volunteers in Mission (UMVIM). He was responsible for coordinating church construction projects, largely manned by volunteers from the United States. Benny, his wife Linda, and teenage twin sons Kevin and K. D. had arrived about the same time the boat was delivered. Bill spent some time teaching Benny how to drive the boat and familiarized him with routine maintenance. Very helpfully, Benny agreed to take over supervision of the boat. Under his direction, the boat was put to use transporting personnel and supplies to outlying areas more easily accessible by water. Bill returned two more times in 1981 to help with maintenance, and Benny Neal became a close friend. Later, Benny played a key role in the direction the Haiti Mission would take.

Almost simultaneously, another event occurred that reshaped the Whites' involvement. During 1980, a controversy arose between Bill and the management of the Atlanta-based firm for which he had worked since 1961. Disagreement over time spent delivering the boat to Haiti and other internal matters caused Bill to decide to leave that company at the end of December to form his own business. Starting a new business generally involves a time of financial and emotional upheaval. For Bill, this was accentuated since son Paul had been involved in business with his father. Paul now became a part of the new company at the same time he and his wife were expecting their first child. To their credit, none of this lessened the Whites' commitment to Haiti.

Formation of the new business did have an interesting side effect. Ironically enough, with little initial profit, the anticipated tax deduction for the gift of the boat was never fully realized. A story that started with a desire to make a tax-wise gift did an about-face and became a story of

Right to left: Alice White, Benny Neal, Giovennes Dieveaux, and Kenneth Bradley on the 1981 fishing expedition of the Pieces of Eight.

spiritual commitment. How curiously interwoven are the material and spiritual affairs of this strange world. Is this something that just happened? Again, I will let you decide.

In spite of the pressures of a new business, Bill managed to return to Haiti twice in 1981 to help maintain the boat. However, his practical mind also began to think of additional ways the boat might be used to benefit the people. A familiar proverb seemed to make sense: "Give a hungry man a fish and he eats today and is hungry tomorrow. Give him a hook and he will eat every day." With hunger a prevalent concern and Bill a fisherman, why not make use of the boat to teach the people how to fish and thereby help alleviate hunger?

And so, with a plane loaded with fishing gear, Bill and Alice left Charlotte two days after Christmas 1981 to launch an exploratory fishing trip. Benny Neal, his twin sons Kevin and K. D., and Dieveaux, the Haitian caretaker of the boat, joined them. While the trip was interesting and challenging, it did not prove productive, and the results were disappointing. Very few fish were caught, so a second trip was planned for April of 1982.

This trip was carefully researched and a specific plan for the development of a fishing co-op was submitted to the Haitian Church, to UMCOR,

Bill White loads their plane for one of its many trips to Haiti.

and to the Board of Global Ministries. Everyone was excited about this possibility and urged Bill to proceed. If the plan proved feasible, the possibility of some start-up money seemed realistic. Then, for the first time, Bill shared his plans with Providence United Methodist Church and asked if they would be a part of this venture.

From its inception, Providence Church has had a reputation for mission involvement. At the organizing conference, when the church was officially started, a "mission special" was approved even before a pastor was appointed. This church, itself a product of the Charlotte District Mission Society, was born with a determination to be involved in mission outreach. However, as buildings had to be financed and staff enlarged, less discretionary money was available, and the vision for mission assumed a lesser priority in the operating budget. Still, there was a significant group of persons searching for ways to involve the church in a "hands-on" mission project.

So, the request to Providence Church for help came at an opportune time and met a ready response. At a February meeting, it was decided that some funds received in the Christmas mission offering could be designated for this purpose. A committee, chaired by Al Rose, was appointed to oversee Providence's involvement. The announcement to the congregation read:

> Mr. Kenneth Bradley Jr., a specialist in marine biology, will work as a consultant in this project, along with Bill and Alice White of our church, and Mr. and Mrs. Benny Neal, coordinators for UMCOR in Haiti. The objective is to determine the potential of seafood life and the feasibility of developing fisheries in Haitian waters (operated by the Church) as a food source for Haiti.

The congregation was also given the opportunity to provide supplies and equipment for the trip.

Also encouraged by a warm response from the Reverend Edouard Domond, chairman and superintendent general of the Haitian Methodist Church, and from Dr. Harry Haines and Paul Morton of the General Board of Global Ministries of the United Methodist Church, the expedition began on April 29.

The congregational newsletter at Providence that week contained these words from the pastor.

> Bill and Alice are leaving for a ten day trip to Haiti. They are going because of a dream they share—a dream that one day some of the poorest people in the world will no longer be hungry because they will be eating fish caught from the ocean and made available to them as food.
>
> Other Providence members are also going, not in person, but as we have helped provide supplies and money to make this trip possible. . . . Remember Bill and Alice and the people of Haiti in your prayers. Surround them with your love and concern as we share with them in this venture of faith. . . . Remember, too, that impossible dreams make miracles.

It was at this point that the Haiti Mission of Providence United Methodist Church came into being. It was a wedding of the interest and dreams of Bill and Alice White and the desire of some of the members of Providence for a more direct involvement in missions. The consummation of this union has given birth to many heirs. They have traveled rough roads, gone around many curves, and up and down many hills, but on their journey they have experienced much joy and witnessed many miracles. And the marriage continues.

The fishing trip, though carefully planned, was again a disappointment. The idea, though carefully conceived, was not deemed practical. In spite of all the time and money and effort invested in the project, the report of Dr. Bradley indicated there were too few fish in the area surveyed to make the co-op feasible. In addition, many Haitians, from a predominately agrarian society, were skeptical of fish as a staple food and expressed little desire to venture very far into the ocean. All others involved shared this conclusion. The plan as projected was unworkable. Interestingly enough, this conclusion was confirmed some years later by Jacques Costeau.

If nothing else, this was a good introduction to Haiti. There is a Creole proverb that says, "Beyond mountains, more mountains." Not only does this describe Haiti's vertical geography, but also the historical struggle of its people. Year after year they seem to surmount one obstacle, then encounter another, followed by others. In Haiti one must learn that not every idea, no matter how good it may appear to be, will work. And most assuredly, not every idea that makes sense in this country will find acceptance there. As frustrating as it may be, those wanting to help in Haiti must use resources readily available in that country and conform to the customs and standards of the Haitian people.

As disappointing as it seemed at the time, the effort was not a failure. It left those involved with renewed resolve to find a way to help the people of this strange and enchanting land. It also solidified the desire of Providence Church to support the efforts of Bill and Alice White.

It is this joint commitment to a significant mission that we will explore in the pages ahead.

CHAPTER 4

The "Look-See Mission"

DESPITE DISAPPOINTMENT OVER THE FISHING EXPEDITIONS, BILL AND ALICE REMAINED FIRMLY COMMITTED TO HAITI. IN support of their enthusiasm, several members of Providence Church agreed to pursue other ways in which the church might be involved. Benny Neal offered a suggestion. Why not bring a small group to Haiti to look over several mission sites and see if any might be a place to get involved? This idea had worked for others, and it had been given a name. Not surprisingly, it was called a "Look-See Mission."

This seemed to be a reasonable proposal, so eight persons were recruited who would pay their way and take the trip. Benny Neal agreed to arrange lodging and ground transportation in Haiti. So, on December 27, 1982, seven persons boarded an Eastern Airlines flight at the Charlotte airport and departed for Port-au-Prince, via Miami. The pastor followed the next day.

In early 1982 Bill had purchased a different airplane that could accommodate an additional three hundred pounds of supplies for his frequent Haiti trips. Now, with two engines, he even felt comfortable taking passengers along. So on December 27, the Whites flew to Leesburg, Florida, and picked up their son-in-law Dick Daily, who accompanied them on the flight to Haiti.

The full group, totaling eleven, included the Whites, Daily, Rev. and Mrs. Dickson (Harley and Inez), Howard and Carolyn Boylan, Ed and Dottie Johnson, and Al and Helen Rose. Benny Neal had arranged accommodations at the Lay Training Center at Fréres near Port-au-Prince. The dormitory, not being used during the holidays, offered sleeping space and cooking equipment. With men and women in separate quarters on bunk beds, the facilities were adequate but spartan. There was no hot water, no screens, and no mosquito netting, but mosquito coils did burn all night. Though not exactly suited for a luxury winter vacation in the Caribbean, it was satisfactory.

Pure water was purchased in five-gallon jugs, and the group did its own meal preparation. Breakfast was in simple continental style. Sandwiches were prepared for takeout at lunch, but the evening meals were superb. Each family brought the fixin's from home for one dinner meal. Amazingly enough, all the food made it through customs without a problem. However, the group still remembers Ed Johnson racing through the Miami airport with a carry-on bag in one hand and a dish of lasagna balanced in the other.

And so we arrived at what Robert and Nancy Heinl, in their book *Written in Blood*, described as a "place of beauty, romance, mystery, kindness, humor, selfishness, betrayal, cruelty, bloodshed, hunger and poverty." Close to six million people are crowded into this land, roughly the size of the state of Maryland, with only 13 percent of its land area worth cultivating. It did not surprise us to learn that the average income for the country was only $175 per year.

Wanting to assist in some tangible way and not feel we were only sightseeing, the group made a decision to be involved in at least one helpful undertaking. Choosing one that could be accomplished with limited skills, we committed the first day to a painting project at the Methodist Clinic of LaSaline, operated by Sister Paulette Holley. Donning old clothes, the group picked up brushes, rollers, and paint at the remarkable hardware store run by Mr. Jean Angus, a member of the Port-au-Prince Methodist Church, and went to work.

So intense was the effort that when Helen Rose became nauseous, she was simply placed on an examination table, covered with a sheet so as not to get splattered with paint, and left there to recover. An uninformed visitor might well have mistaken this room for a morgue.

The concentrated effort paid off. At the end of the day, the entire inside of the clinic had a fresh coat of paint. Sister Paulette was profuse in her expressions of gratitude and then added, "This is great. Most volunteer groups only paint one room."

Tired, but satisfied, the group departed with a deep appreciation for what they observed on their first mission visit. Here in the heart of the crowded and bustling city of Port-au-Prince was a church sanctuary, a school with an enrollment of 350 children, and a medical and dental clinic treating 35,000 patients a year. It was a remarkable beginning for an exciting "Look-See Mission."

A fourteen-passenger van, supplied by Benny Neal, provided great transportation, so the week proceeded comfortably with several other

Benny Neal (second from right) talks to the "Look-See Mission" group in 1982.

visits. The general superintendent of the Eglisé Methodiste d'Haiti met the group at the College Bird Church (the "Mother Church" of Haitian Methodism). Methodism came to this country from Britain in 1817 and continued for 150 years as a part of the British Methodist Church. In 1967 it became a part of the independent Methodist Churches of the Caribbean and the Americas (MCCA). The superintendent shared helpful information about the activities of this and other churches of Haiti. Later in the week the group joined this congregation in their New Year's Eve Watchnight worship service.

To the west, in Petit Goave, a visit was made to the Christian Institute for Rural Life. Operated for many years by Brother Marco Depestre, this mission provided excellent models of self-help ministry, teaching Haitians new skills in their fight to overcome poverty. Interesting examples included solar cookers, waste disposal facilities, cisterns, irrigation systems, and fish ponds. This is a long-standing and successful mission endeavor.

Another day was the occasion for a tour of the Baptist Mission. Organized in 1943 by a Baptist minister from the United States, it too provided an example of Christian ministry, not only caring for souls but also helping people help themselves to relieve problems of malnutrition, poverty, and illiteracy. There was also an opportunity to visit the *Pieces of Eight* and see the gift boat serving the people of Haiti.

However, the most significant excursion of the week was to the Cap Haitien area in the northern part of Haiti. Isolated from Port-au-Prince by a five-hour drive over rough and crooked mountain roads filled with potholes, Cap Haitien seemed impossible to reach by automobile. However, Bill filled his airplane to capacity with the six men and flew to Cap Haitien, landing at the small unimproved airport after several cows had been shooed off the runway. The Reverend Ed Holmes, the British-born pastor of the Cap Haitian Circuit, met us and spent the rest of the day giving a tour of much of the area covered by the nine Methodist churches in his parish. This jaunt in his English Land Rover was quick, but helpful, and provided a great deal of information in a short period of time. It was also an introduction to a sincere and hardworking pastor who had a very clear vision of what he wanted to see happen.

Like most Haitian pastors, he was committed to a multifaceted ministry serving the total needs of his parishioners. Reinforcing his philosophy, he made a profound and memorable statement as we bounced along the rough roads. Al Rose recalled it this way, "The challenge here is how do I preach and teach the love of Jesus Christ to these people when they are hungry and hurting so? We've got to find a way to solve these problems first." His vision focused on making each church on the circuit a center of activity for its community. This would include a church sanctuary for worship, a school to educate the children, a well to provide pure water, a clinic to provide health care, and persons who could teach the people to improve their methods of growing food.

Some church buildings were already in place, but most needed significant repairs. A new sanctuary was needed at Dondon and at Latannerie, and all needed a deep well with pure water. Because of Ed's experience with a medical clinic in his former pastorate at Jeremie, he was focused in his determination to build clinics at Dondon, Latannerie, and Tovar. He also considered a tract of bottomland near Cap Haitien, owned by the Methodist Church, to be a useful place for agricultural experiments. Ed was a gifted communicator, so he was able to articulate his vision clearly.

Because of its distance from Port-au-Prince and because this poor rural area had difficulty attracting funding, few volunteer mission teams had come to Cap Haitien in recent years. Benny Neal, however, informed us that Ed was uncovering new sources of funding and would be willing to welcome building and medical teams. Quickly, Ed let us know that if we would come we would be welcome. Then he began telling us, in practical terms, how this could work.

Ed's contagious enthusiasm started our minds racing, thinking about ways Providence United Methodist Church might participate in the vision shared with us by this charismatic personality. Yes, we acknowledged, we did have persons with engineering and construction backgrounds who should be willing to volunteer time and expertise to help with his building projects. This certainly proved to be the case.

Equally, if not more important, was the fact that Providence, being the suburban church it is, had a large pool of persons with medical training—doctors, dentists, pharmacists, nurses, lab assistants, technicians, drug salesmen, and others—who could get involved in helping the medical clinics. Other than an occasional missionary doctor, a few midwives, and the local Voodoo priest, no medical services were easily available to any of his rural parishioners, and Ed wanted to change that.

Could we help? Why not? we reflected. Strangely, and even without our being aware of it, a consensus developed. This was the place for Providence to be. We knew we could help with repairs and construction. We were also confident in our ability to provide people and supplies to help Ed's dream for the clinics become reality.

Of course we would not be alone. Others were already involved. The Methodist Church has always been a connectional church, doing together what we cannot do alone. UMCOR, through the General Board of Global Ministries, was at work with Advance Special offerings supporting funding for Haiti. Construction volunteers from the Western North Carolina Conference of the United Methodist Church had worked in mission areas throughout the world. Several other conferences across the country were potential partners. Ed and the Haitian Church would be in charge and fully supportive, but what we had to offer would mesh well with these other efforts. This was a place to be involved. This was a fit.

Upon our return to Port-au-Prince, the events of the day were shared with the rest of the group. Their response was equally enthusiastic, especially that of Alice. Without knowing it, her growing knowledge of nursing was already preparing her to play a key role in the fulfillment of this vision. Did this just happen? By now I'm convinced it was more providential. But please, don't let me make up your mind for you.

And so our vision was born. We would join with Ed Holmes and the Methodists of the Cap Haitian Circuit in an effort to provide buildings and staff medical clinics in the north of Haiti. We knew we could, and we knew we would.

We now needed to go home and articulate this vision so that the members of Providence Church would want to use their money and their skill to help implement the dream. We were anxious to move ahead. As soon as possible, we wanted to return to Haiti and get started.

CHAPTER 5

The First Steps

A LONG JOURNEY USUALLY BEGINS WITH SMALL STEPS. AND SO IT WAS. THE HAITI "LOOK-SEE MISSION" GROUP WAS established as an ad hoc committee, determined to involve the church and get something under way. Unlike some committees, they did just that. A large task lay ahead. There was money to raise, people to recruit, and multitudinous details to be worked out. But they were ready to get started.

All of this was on the table at the first meeting. However another concern rose to the top of the priority list—pure water for Dondon. Al Rose recalled their experience in Haiti. They had closed the doors and shutters and gone inside the church building so as not to have to eat their bagged lunches in front of a large crowd, curious, and obviously hungry. Let Al tell it:

> As we ate, Ed Holmes asked us to share our professional lives, what we did for a living. When Bill White described his engineering specialty in water purification and waste treatment, Ed was overjoyed. He proceeded to describe in detail the horrible water conditions there. The people of Dondon got their water either from a polluted stream, or from a shallow well on the church premises, located adjacent to the public latrine.
>
> Everyone well remembered how Bill White, improvising with twine and bottles, gathered samples of the well water. Then miraculously he was able to "smuggle" these through customs and back to his lab in Charlotte. Now at the Committee meeting he confirmed that, yes

indeed, "The well water showed contamination that could become dangerous if a septic drain field was ever placed in service near the current well." And, that the water contained high quantities of ferric iron which is what turned their teeth "black" when people drank from the well.

Two solutions were possible. First, a simple treatment plant could be built. However, since this required careful daily maintenance, it did not seem feasible. Secondly, a deep well could be drilled with a casing going below the iron-bearing strata.

Could a well be dug? Probably, but who would do it? Was there a well-drilling rig in Cap Haitien? If so, would it be possible to get it across the rough terrain and up to Dondon? On top of that, what would it cost? The meeting adjourned without reaching any conclusions.

However, over the next few weeks two things happened to move this discussion forward. First, knowing that money would be needed, Al Rose approached the chair of the Finance Committee to discuss the matter. Leroy Robinson then acknowledged that, strange as it might seem in a Methodist church, a small surplus of eight thousand had been carried forward from the 1982 operating budget. "Was any of this available for use for a mission to Haiti?" Al asked. Together it was agreed that a figure of

Bill White, Ed Holmes, and Dick Daily (back to camera) check out the "old" Dondon well.

three thousand dollars might be reasonable, and so this amount was set aside for use in Haiti.

Shortly thereafter the second event occurred. On Easter Sunday, April 3, 1983, a full-page feature article appeared in the *Richmond Times-Dispatch* under the title "Bringing Hope to Haiti." Knowing of Bill's interest in this country, his mother, who lived in Richmond, clipped the story and mailed it to him.

Betty Pettinger, staff writer, compared the luxury of life in Virginia with conditions that Easter in Haiti. There, she observed, "Some people will drink and bathe themselves in fetid ditch water, some will go dirty and thirsty, and those with good clear water will carefully consider the use of every drop." She went on to report that Jack Hancox had given up his pastorate at a Southern Baptist church in Fredericksburg, Virginia, and, along with his wife Donna, had moved to Haiti to work under the sponsorship of the Baptist Mission Board. With the help of a $100,000 grant from that group, Jack had bought a well-drilling truck and was primarily involved in boring wells. And, he was doing it at a cost well below the price charged by commercial firms.

Immediately, Al and Bill began making telephone calls to Port-au-Prince. It wasn't long before they had Jack on the phone. Yes, he was drilling wells. No, he was not anywhere near Dondon, but he would be before long, and when that happened he would be glad to get back with them.

And what would it cost? Nothing for the drilling rig and only cost for materials used, plus fifty dollars per day for the Haitian labor. "Probably about three thousand dollars," Jack said. The exact amount promised by the Finance Committee a few days earlier. Did all of this *just happen*? What do you think?

With a well now assured, another question arose. How would the people get the water to the surface? Without electricity, a hand pump would be needed and these were not cheap. It was only a short time later that Jack Hancox called Al to report on his progress and also said he felt sure that an India Marco II pump could be obtained from UNICEF, the United Nations organization associated with trick-or-treat offerings at Halloween. Then, with just a couple of other calls, a hand pump was on its way to Dondon. By now it should be no surprise to learn that it was free, costing the mission nothing, thanks to all those nickels and dimes contributed during Halloween.

Projects seldom move quickly in Haiti, so it was some time before the well was completed. However, with this amazing confluence of ecumenical efforts between Methodists, Baptists, and UNICEF, pure water was guaranteed. The first step had been taken toward having a medical clinic at Dondon.

Al Rose later reported:

> I don't have the ability to express my personal feelings when I returned to Dondon. To stand there and see the smiles on the faces of children pumping water, women filling large containers of water and then loading them atop their heads to carry back to their huts, or a woman stooping with an entire stalk of bananas balanced on her head, to take a dipper of water to quench her thirst, couldn't help but make me a believer in miracles. Don't you agree?

Al got a spectacular photograph of the well showing two Haitian boys, one pumping and the other drinking from the spigot. This has become the unofficial symbol and logo of the Haiti Mission of Providence United Methodist Church. Used in a variety of ways, the framed photo also hangs in many homes where it serves as a daily reminder of this miracle of water at Dondon.

Nineteen eighty-three was a busy year. Sharing its story, the ad hoc committee talked with anyone who would listen. Many were already receptive. The boat stories and the fishing expeditions had attracted interest from many quarters. Talk about the well aroused new interest.

Children celebrate the new well at Dondon. This Al Rose photo became the unofficial logo of the Haiti Mission.

Chaired by Howard Boylan, a "Look-See Mission" participant, the church's Outreach Commission also had a ready-made stake in what happened. Al Rose reported regularly to them, keeping them informed as plans developed.

To fully understand this story, one must remember its historical perspective. During this post-Vietnam period many mainline churches downgraded their emphasis on erecting buildings and made mission outreach a priority. This was a philosophy accepted by many Methodists, as well as other denominations. An Episcopal church just up the street from Providence made headlines when they delayed a major building program and instead raised $2 million for their "Matthew 25 Fund." This was money devoted entirely to mission causes.

The Providence Outreach Commission itself was extremely active. Catching this same spirit, it sought to earmark at least 25 percent of the church's annual operating budget for missions. The early 1980s proved to be the period when the church became involved in many new outreach programs, most of which still continue. Included among these were involvement with the Crisis Assistance Ministry, Friendship Trays (meal delivery to the homebound), International House, Shepherds Center, and the Sunday blood donors program for the Red Cross. Projects begun specifically by Providence included the Bethlehem Center Weekend Meals Program, the Tutoring Program at Cotswold Elementary School, the Prison Books Program, and Medi-Help, a storeroom for used medical equipment to be loaned without cost.

The Haiti project was warmly accepted as well. Of course, not everyone jumped on this particular bandwagon, but the idea did not fall on deaf ears. With anticipation for the development of a Providence team, the ad hoc committee was able to gain the approval of forty-five hundred dollars in the 1984 operating budget. This line item, now greatly increased, has remained a part of the annual budget ever since.

Meanwhile, a great deal went on in Haiti. In March of 1983 the ideas for Dondon and Tovar projected by Ed Holmes received the approval by the Haitian Church and were added to the official list of UMCOR projects authorized to receive Advance Special offerings from United Methodists. As this list was publicized, groups from across the United States began to respond with money and volunteer teams.

UMCOR involvement in Haiti did not begin until 1967 when the Haitian Church became a part of the Methodist Churches of the Caribbean and the Americas (MCCA). Its first financial support went to repair damage from a series of hurricanes. Early support mostly targeted other areas of the country, but with Ed Holmes's arrival, the Cap Haitien Circuit began to get its share. The period between 1980 and the beginning of the revolution in 1986 proved to be the "glory days" for outside support for the north of Haiti. Several volunteer construction and medical teams made their way to the area during that time.

It was primarily to Dondon, but also to Tovar, that Providence Church directed its first efforts. Conversation and correspondence went back and forth and on June 24, 1983, Bill White received a letter from Paul Morton, secretary for Specialized Ministries at UMCOR. His letter included comments such as these:

> I am happy that you and your church have become interested and involved in Haiti. As you know, Haiti needs all the help it can get. Also, I'm very happy you have become involved in the Cap Haitien area. You certainly could not find anyone better to work with than Ed Holmes. He is just absolutely tops.

> Ed Holmes and Edouard Domond (Chairman and General Superintendent of the Haitian Church) wrote me about the project to build a new sanctuary at Dondon, and make the old church into a clinic. That is a project that's approved by the Haitian Church and is also approved by UMCOR. Whenever it is ready to be built we certainly will be supportive of your church doing the building or revamping the church into a clinic.

With regard to clinics he added:

> The Haitian Church is in the process of trying to build a system of rural clinics. . . . I feel the church there has a real commitment toward health care for the people, and I think the clinic at Dondon is an excellent project for you. I have every confidence in the world that it will be utilized fully, particularly if you folks support it and back it in its beginning years.

Now, only six months after the "Look-See Mission," Providence was free to move ahead. Only the details remained. There was money to be raised, construction plans to be drawn, people to be recruited, and logistics developed so all of this could be accomplished, with volunteers, and in a limited time period. And, most importantly, it had to be done in the spirit clearly outlined by Paul Morton in this same letter.

> It's very important that the clinic is owned and operated by the local people and the Methodist Church of Haiti. Your work and your help are supplemental to them and you are there under their direction. This is extremely important so that the clinic will continue even if somewhere

down the road you folks lose interest. They need to sense and have a feeling of ownership—that it is their responsibility to carry it on with supplemental help from people like you.

In this spirit, and with renewed commitment, the Haiti Mission Committee forged ahead, now ready to make concrete plans. Money, of course, was a formidable obstacle to overcome. With the cost of work at Dondon estimated at around $30,000, the 1984 Providence Church budget amount of $4,500 looked mighty small. That would barely be a starting point. What could they do? Two things happened to make this doable—and more.

It did not go well for the *Pieces of Eight* after Benny Neal completed his term in Haiti in mid-1983 and returned to the United States. His replacement was not asked to take over supervision of the boat. With little service or maintenance, deterioration quickly set in and usage declined sharply.

Seeking its best utilization, the Haitian Church decided to lease the vessel to a hotel in Port-au-Prince for use with its guests. This worked well for awhile and provided a helpful source of revenue. Everyone was pleased until a church official made a routine inspection and found empty liquor bottles in various and sundry places on the boat. With its extremely strong stand against alcoholic beverages of any kind, the Haitian Church made the quick decision to cancel the hotel lease at the earliest possible date.

Remaining idle and without proper care, the *Pieces of Eight* would soon be unserviceable. So an appeal went out to Bill White. What can we do? What do you recommend? While it was no longer his boat, they still looked to him for help.

After lengthy conversations, it seemed that the best alternative was to sell the boat. Al Rose then reached an agreement with Edouard Domond that Providence Church would act as agent to sell the boat for the Haitian Church. Twenty percent of the proceeds of the sale would go to the Methodist Church in Port-au-Prince and 80 percent would be fully committed to the UMCOR-approved project for the construction of a sanctuary and other related projects at Dondon. The Outreach Commission of Providence United Methodist Church then authorized a group to go to Port-au-Prince (at their own expense) to find the best way to make this happen. The commission also authorized up to three thousand dollars from the 1984 budget to be used for any necessary repairs.

On June 22, 1984, Bill White, Howard Boylan, Doug Bowers, and Benny Neal (now living in the United States) left for Port-au-Prince in Bill's airplane. Al Rose, flying commercially, joined them there. Upon arrival they went to the dock area to survey what repairs might be needed. Some work was necessary, but the motor and drive shafts were in good condition. About five hundred dollars for batteries, replacement parts, and supplies would make the boat operable.

Two options for its sale seemed possible. The boat could be taken to Miami, restored to peak condition, and bring a sizeable sum. However the expenses for accomplishing this, along with a hefty sales commission, would be enormous. The other choice was to make the necessary repairs and try to find a buyer in Haiti. While this was a long shot, it seemed worth a try. It was agreed that the easiest and best choice, if possible, would be to sell the boat in Haiti for $15,000.

The first day was spent on engine repair and caulking. The second day the boat was taken to a sandbar in the bay where the hull was cleaned. Everything appeared to be in satisfactory working order.

By now I hope you are beginning to believe in miracles because a native Haitian, Mr. Volel, appeared on the dock and inquired, "Is the boat for sale?" The answer of course was, "Yes!" A day later, after discussion and negotiation, an offer was tendered. Determining that indeed the prospective buyer did have cash to buy the boat, the Providence group accepted his offer, which was confirmed by Haitian Church officials. The amount—$15,000!

Counting on the possible use of 1985 budget funds, about $20,000 of Providence's goal was now in sight. While this was still not nearly enough, the goal seemed much more attainable.

Yet another happening dovetailed with the sale of the boat. The Reverend Cliff Lamb, from Houston, Texas, got in touch with Ed Holmes. He had seen the list of approved projects on the UMCOR list and expressed an interest in bringing a Texas team of volunteers to build the sanctuary at Dondon. He had enough money and volunteers to do this project as well as another project in Port-au-Prince. Ed Holmes contacted Bill White, and it was agreed that Cliff's group would do the sanctuary. Providence was now free to focus its efforts on rebuilding the old church so it could be converted into a clinic.

This worked well. It was the clinic that most interested Providence anyway. Now they had the money to do the job at Dondon with enough left over to be able to set their sights on building a clinic at Tovar as well. This turn of events combined their dual interest in construction and in medical involvement. Providence, now firmly committed to a medical mission effort, looked forward to building, staffing, and supporting not one, but two clinics.

The rest of 1984 was devoted to putting together a team of volunteers who could begin these efforts in January of 1985. These months were also a time of transition, with a change of pastors taking place at Providence Church. The Reverend Larry Wilkinson was assigned as the new senior minister of the church and began his duties on September 1. This proved to be a good choice by the bishop. Larry threw his full support behind the project and became a member of the first team himself. Fully devoted to this effort, he returned four times in subsequent years. Even after moving to another parish in 1990, he continued to recruit volunteers for the Haiti Mission from his new church.

By Christmas of 1984, exactly five years from the time Bill White announced that he was giving his boat to the church, Providence was poised and ready for this new venture.

CHAPTER 6

A Time to Prepare

IF YOU ARE NOT DIRECTLY INVOLVED, IT IS DIFFICULT TO ENVISION THE ENORMOUS AMOUNT OF PLANNING NEEDED to prepare teams for a volunteer mission effort. Many suggestions and guidelines, based on the experience of other Methodists, were available in 1984. However, handling the details was the responsibility of the Haiti Mission Committee of Providence United Methodist Church.

For them, 1984 was a very busy year. Dates for the trip were established. Additional financial support was secured for the project and also for its volunteers. Transportation plans, to and from Haiti, had to be scheduled and provisions made for food and for comfortable and safe lodging. Ground transportation in Haiti was arranged, and, since the native language is Creole, a few interpreters were lined up. And of course, construction and medical volunteers had to be recruited.

At first it seemed that three teams would be needed to do the work, but after assessing the interest of potential volunteers, it was decided that two teams would be more realistic. After several conversations with the Haitian Church, the committee found a time that did not conflict with visits by other volunteer teams. Finally, firm dates were set for January 1–12 and January 16–26, 1985.

The objective for the first building team was to remove the roof of the old sanctuary at Dondon, build new trusses, and, if possible, put them in place. The second group would then complete the roof and do inside renovations. If any time remained, they would start on the new building for the Tovar Clinic.

Reenforcing its firm commitment to medical work, the committee also determined that medical personnel would be included as a part of each team. Both of these objectives proved to be realistic.

Five thousand dollars was in the 1984 Providence Church budget and another five thousand dollars projected for 1985. With the proceeds from the sale of the boat in a Haitian Church account in Port-au-Prince, specifically designated for use at Dondon and Tovar, funding was pretty well assured. However, two issues remained to be addressed.

The first involved a key principle accepted as a part of almost every volunteer mission effort—volunteers were expected to pay for their own transportation, food, lodging, and other related costs. Going to Haiti was not to be viewed as a free vacation trip. Church members interested in the project were invited to consider one of the following options:

- Go and pay your way
- Pay so someone else can go, or
- Go with scholarship help

While some do receive scholarship help from others, church members or participants always pay the travel costs.

A second issue was crucial. Funds of this nature must be accounted for properly; this is certainly important from the church's perspective. In addition, since mission travel of this nature is usually considered by the Internal Revenue Service to be a tax-deductible expense, good records are doubly important.

Complete reports of all receipts and expenditures, both in the church and in White and Co., where many of the details have been handled, is a matter of record. Over the years, the church has received and disbursed funds to the Haiti Mission, and church officials always have been satisfied that these monies are accounted for in a reliable way.

With the financial concerns handled, the matter of logistics moved to the forefront. *Webster's Unabridged Dictionary* defines logistics as "the branch of military science having to do with moving, supplying, and quartering troops." Substitute the word "volunteers" for "troops" and you have an accurate description of what took place in 1984, and what is repeated each time a Haiti Mission team is organized.

First, air transportation was scheduled. Unfortunately, no major airline flew to Cap Haitien, but Port-au-Prince, seven hundred miles southeast of Miami, was a regular stop for Eastern Airlines. Ticketing passengers from Charlotte to Miami and then to Haiti was relatively simple.

Food and lodging was more difficult to arrange. A few hardy people on teams from other conferences camped out, but this certainly limited the number of potential volunteers. Camping would never work at Providence.

Dinner at the Beck Hotel.

It must be remembered that getting from Port-au-Prince to Cap Haitien involves a five- or six-hour trip, so an overnight stay in Port-au-Prince was required at the beginning and end of the trip. Lodging at the Coconut Villa Hotel was easily arranged since Bill and Alice had stayed there on earlier trips. But it was a different matter in Cap Haitien.

After a good bit of research, the Beck Hotel was selected. Built in 1952 by a family of German origin, the current owner had been a part of the operation from the beginning. The hotel met all the needs for the Haiti Mission teams of Providence—cost, convenience, comfort, accessibility, safety, and very importantly, good food service. Food prepared under the direction of Mr. Beck, and with his recipes, was excellent. Some say it was not exactly like home, but close enough to satisfy all but the most finicky eater.

"Pure water" was a special bonus. Travelers to most places have to depend on bottled water, but not at the Beck Hotel. A capped spring atop a mountain on the hotel property provided water that was quite drinkable. No known cases of "Haitian Happiness" could be traced to this source. And containers of water from the hotel were carried to the work sites, eliminating concerns about drinking water. Also providing plenty of space to store materials and preparing packed lunches, these accommodations were ideal. So much so, they are still used by the Providence Haiti Mission.

While it was not a big concern for the first team, a major task of later mission trips has involved shipping materials to Haiti ahead of time. Many of the needs (building, food, and medical) are simply not available in that country. While not typical, the 1991 trip required packing ninety-two boxes weighing 1,751 pounds and shipping them six weeks ahead of the scheduled team's arrival. Most teams require the shipment of fifty to sixty boxes of supplies.

So much for the problem of supplying the volunteers, but what about moving them? Getting to Port-au-Prince would be simple, but traveling the road to Cap Haitien was tough. The daylong trip over a "paved" road with more than numerous potholes made for a very rough ride. Fortunately, the Haitian Church had access to a Mercedes truck. While not very comfortable, it got the job done. A daily round-trip ride from the hotel to Dondon or Tovar added a one-and-a-half to two-hour rough ride each day—this time over unpaved roads. Just getting to the work site involved strenuous exercise.

With the addition of a few interpreters, the logistics were pretty well taken care of. Now the recruiting could begin in earnest. Al Rose and Howard Boylan were put in charge of producing a simple brochure to distribute to the congregation. This fact sheet encouraged members to be a work team member, be a medical specialist on a team, or help underwrite work team costs.

For the building teams, minimal but important skills were needed:

- Hammer nails
- Operate paint brush
- Carry water bucket
- Shovel dirt
- Operate handsaw

More than minimal tasks required more skills:

- General carpentry
- General masonry
- Read blueprints

The project was portrayed as "an act of love and care from the people of Providence to establish a growing concern for others." Clearly explained also was the expectation that volunteers were to be fully supportive of Haitian Christians and to be effective witnesses for the United Methodist Church.

It is not easy to leave the comforts of home and go to a strange and scary place. In addition, it would be a strenuous trip requiring a lot of physical labor. But in part due to the excellent arrangements which had been made and even more to the challenge to be part of something worthwhile, the people responded. By December, twenty hardy recruits had signed on, agreeing to be trailblazers for this first effort. And scores of others have followed in their footsteps.

It is never enough to enlist a team of volunteers. There has to be work ready to do and tools and supplies to do it with. With Bill White in charge of construction details, this part went well. During his visit in June, Bill consulted with Ed Holmes about the Dondon Clinic, and by taking measurements and photos he was able to do the designs in Charlotte. By December, detailed drawings had been made and approved by the Haitian Church. In his meticulous way, Bill also provided a bill of materials listing the exact number of two by fours, pieces of plywood, and the amount of concrete blocks, cement, sand, and other materials that would be needed. Even the nails were not forgotten.

With only five or six days to do the actual work, it was crucial that everything be in readiness. So by mid-December the list was in Ed Holmes's hands. He would have materials on the site when the first crews arrived and also arrange for several Haitians to be there to help with carpentry and masonry.

Alice was also busy. Sites were identified for medical work, and arrangements made to have supplies and drugs on hand. A dentist was recruited to go with the first team and an ophthalmologist with the second. For these first trips, only very basic treatment was to be offered, and most instruments were carried along as hand luggage. Later medical teams, with more ambitious goals, required extensive planning and shipping of large amounts of equipment, supplies, and drugs well in advance.

The Haitian Ministry of Health has always been, and still is, very strict in their requirement that all medical personnel be licensed, and copies of their credentials have to be in the hands of the Haitian officials well in advance of their visit. It was Alice who made sure this was done and approved.

Here again, Ed Holmes handled details on the Haiti end. Work sites, for the dentist and doctor, were identified at Dondon, at Tovar, and at Latannerie. There would be specific places where they could see patients and do their work.

By mid-December recruiting was complete, and a final orientation session was held on December 18. Using a printed list of instructions, everyone was briefed on travel plans, passports, suggested immunizations, health cautions, money needs, and clothing recommendations. Each job was outlined and preliminary work assignments were given.

Information about Haiti and its people was discussed, as well as their responsibilities as visitors to the country. Again, they were reminded that they were to be supportive of their Haitian brothers and sisters and be effective witnesses for the United Methodist Church. The closing line in their instruction sheet read: "Go with an open mind. You are not there to save Haiti. You are there to share your Christian experience. The Haitian people are very proud. They are a free democratic nation. You will learn from them, and they will learn from you."

In this spirit two teams were now ready for their mission. A prayer, written by Jeanette Goodhand and given at a December worship service, would send them on their way.

> O Thou who rules by thy providence our land and sea, defend, guide, and bless all messengers of Christ—in danger be their shield, in darkness be their hope. Enrich their word and work with wisdom, joy, and power.
>
> We ask thee especially to follow with thy favor and thy protecting care those, our friends, who this week leave for Haiti to serve as your ambassadors. Sustain them in weariness and pain.
>
> May the work of their hands, matched by the meditations of their hearts, be an inspiration to the people with whom they come into contact. And, may the fruits of their labors be seen in the fullness of time.
>
> In Jesus' name we pray. Amen.

CHAPTER 7

The Trailblazers

IN JANUARY OF 1985 TWO TEAMS BLAZED A TRAIL THAT, FOR FIFTEEN YEARS, OTHERS HAVE FOLLOWED. SIX MEMBERS OF the original "Look-See Mission" participated, and eleven new volunteers joined them. They set out with specific long-range goals in mind:

- Complete the Dondon Clinic
- Build the Tovar Clinic
- Provide treatment by volunteer medical personnel
- Arrange for local nurses to staff both clinics on a regular basis

In support of these goals some members of each team were involved in construction work. The first team focused on remodeling the old sanctuary at Dondon, getting it ready to be used as a medical clinic. The second group worked there, but also was called on to help Rev. Ed Holmes do repairs at several other locations.

Faithful to the vision of providing health services in this area, a dentist (Dr. Fred Miller) was included on the first team and an eye doctor (Dr. Walter Bullington) on the second. Their beginning efforts were modest but extremely important. Since that time, at least one team has visited Haiti every year, and each one has included medical personnel. What these pioneers did provided a model for later groups to use and improve on. So, let's take a closer look.

Team I departed Charlotte on January 1, flew to Miami, and then to Port-au-Prince. After an overnight stay at the Coconut Villa they departed early the next day by Mercedes truck. After a rough five-hour ride, observing people in a mostly desolate mountainous region eking out a bare existence, they arrived in Cap Haitien in time for a late lunch.

They were surprised and pleased with their accommodations. In her journal Carol Brown described it this way. "The Hotel Beck overlooks the bay and . . . provides for us much beyond my expectations. The food far outweighed anything I could have asked for." To support this observation, she listed the menus for the first day:

> Lunch: Country fried steak, green peas, French fries, and for dessert, a mango dish

> Dinner: Marinated beef, boiled potatoes, okra, tomatoes and onions, and for dessert, vanilla pudding

One of the reasons volunteers from this country are able to endure the rigors of a work team in Haiti, and keep going back, is the safe haven provided by the Beck Hotel. While not a five-star accommodation by any measure, it has been more than acceptable.

The first evening for Team I (and later for Team II) was spent with the superintendent of the Cap Haitien Circuit, the Reverend Ed Holmes. Ed provided gracious words of welcome and an orientation which served to make everyone feel comfortable about relating to a new people and a new environment.

Very early on Thursday morning, loaded with workers and supplies, the Mercedes truck and Ed Holmes's Land Rover began the bumpy one-hour ride over the narrow mountain road leading to Dondon. This group included Dr. Miller and his helpers (who did their first day's work at Dondon) and the construction workers.

The construction crew, under the direction of Rev. Larry Wilkinson, spent each of their six working days at Dondon. Upon his return home Larry's report in the Providence newsletter was brief but descriptive: "Team I (Al Rose, Kathy Williams, Susan and John Jordan, and Larry Wilkinson) built eleven (11) roof trusses, stained them with used motor oil, erected them on the building walls, and readied the roof for the installation of the tin roofing."

Their work was a bit more complex than this description and involved full days and a heavy work schedule. With Bill White's detailed blueprints in hand, the crew went to work immediately. There was no electricity, but a rented gasoline-powered generator was brought so that power tools could be used to cut the wood for the trusses. Following Bill's pattern, and laying out the pieces on the open ground, they were able to do an effective job.

You might be wondering about the used motor oil. So did the crew. But Ed Holmes, with his English background and a concern about termites, insisted that each piece of the trusses be rubbed with the dirty oil. It was a messy job. One day following his cold shower, and after a hard day sliding around on the dirty trusses, Howard Boylan was heard to say, "My buns are black!" Bill White later learned that termites were not a problem in this region. So a decision about motor oil was made—never again!

A construction project may seem simple, but in Haiti it rarely is. When Team I left Dondon the roof was nearly complete. But one week later when Team II arrived, they discovered that Haitian workers had misunderstood their role, and materials to be used for scaffolding had been used to build something different. Team II had to spend their first day undoing, before they could begin doing. This was a good lesson in patience, for few things happen in Haiti exactly the way they are planned. Volunteers almost always experience ups and downs, and only perseverance will get the job done.

Construction Team II (consisting of Bill White, Doug Bowers, Wilton and Mary Dee Parr, Howard and Carolyn Boylan, and Inez Dickson) found this to be true. It became necessary for them to adjust their schedule in order to do what Ed Holmes felt was most important. They *were* able to complete enough of the work at Dondon so that money left behind enabled Haitian crews to finish the project later. But at Ed's request the crew also worked at Plain du Nord doing painting

The well and clinic at Dondon.

Front to back: Mary Dee Parr, Wilton Parr, and Shirley Bullington at Dondon.

and electrical wiring, at Quartier Morin performing the same tasks, and at Tovar laying the foundation for the new clinic. At Tovar everyone got to turn a shovel of dirt for what would become the major project for the next two years.

It was also reported that several amateur painters from this team were observed doing professional-quality paint work on the latrines and chicken houses in some Methodist compounds.

These were long days. One evening, dinner had to be delayed until 8:30 while the group stayed to do their work at Quartier Morin and then (still in their work clothes) participate in the evening prayer service.

The dental team consisted of Dr. Fred Miller (a cousin of Helen Rose) and his wife Susie from Boone, North Carolina. Fred heard about the trip from Al Rose, who also invited him to participate. Carol Brown was pressed into service to keep the instruments clean and the needles filled, and Edy, the Haitian interpreter, chipped in as well. Actually, Edy was allowed to pull two teeth before the week was over. This piqued an interest on Edy's part, and over the years he developed into an able dental assistant.

With no electricity, the dental "clinic" was set up on wooden benches in the open air. This outdoor setting proved effective, and has been the location of choice for most of the dentists who followed. A huge crowd was attracted on the first day. Under these primitive conditions it was not possible to do restorative dentistry, but 110 teeth were pulled. The forty-five patients receiving treatment found much needed relief from their pain and suffering. Each day the dental group visited a new location, returning to Dondon on the final day. For the week, over 400 teeth were pulled. Carol Brown described her participation this way:

> The patients at the clinics were clean, cooperative and friendly. The average person had approximately four teeth pulled. The most pulled was six. Most patients had very large roots, which made pulling the teeth difficult. Fred did a fantastic job with the work, and with the people. His wife Susie (not a dental assistant) did an excellent job as his assistant. I was able to keep the instruments clean and the needles filled. Edy, our interpreter, was good with the people, having their confidence and trust.

It was a good experience for the Millers. Fred said, "We really felt good, but we didn't feel like we scratched the surface. A lot more could be done." And Susie added, "You feel like you really helped. That's why I enjoyed it." To their friends in Boone they reported, "Of all the places we've been, and of all the things we've done, I wish we had done this one before."

The physician for Team II was Dr. Walter Bullington, an ophthalmologist from Charlotte and a member of Providence Church. His wife Shirley, a nurse anesthetist, accompanied him. Alice White was the nurse on the team and Betty Bowers pitched in to keep records. This group became known affectionately as the M.A.S.H. unit.

Walt had been told he did not need to bring along many of his medical instruments. Later he observed, "I could have done more if I had brought more of my equipment." On later trips he did. But even with these limitations he did simple examinations, gave out some medications, and, when helpful, distributed used eyeglasses. I have often wondered how old eyeglasses collected by the Lions Club and others are used. But after seeing what Walt and others were able to do in Haiti, I am a believer. In a place where no other help is available, some that were almost blind are now able to see.

Like the dental team, the M.A.S.H. unit visited five outlying areas including Dondon. Later Walt described it this way:

We put aside all the sophistication of our modern technology to deliver eye care to the people near Cap Haitien. Loading our clinic in boxes on top of the Land Rover, we headed out to outlying villages. Any room will work to deliver the Lord's eye care, but preferably one with a solid roof, window shutters, and doors that work. (Without electricity, this was our lighting system.) Any table and chair makes an ideal examining area. Various pharmaceutical companies or supply houses donated our medical supplies. So you see, with all this available to us, all we needed to have a successful ophthalmology clinic was patients.

Finding patients was no problem in Haiti. The need was great with 237 patients seen that week. On the other hand, many of the eye conditions could not be treated in this setting. Many of the patients Walt saw had problems he could have easily corrected with medicine or with surgery in the United States. Here he was helpless. But Walt was hopeful. "God works in mysterious ways," he said. "Maybe next year he will supply an operating room, and more willing missionaries and volunteers to get the job done."

Fortunately God works with those who have faith. With great frustration over what he could not do, Walt kept returning to Haiti year after year, doing what he could. His patience and perseverance paid off. In 1991 God provided, at last, a place where he could do the surgery for which he was trained.

With Sunday coming in the middle of the work period, each team worshiped in one of the Haitian Methodist churches. Across the years, this has provided a sabbath from hard work and a meaningful worship experience. It also has been a time for bonding and developing a relationship between team members and local Christians.

To the trailblazers, the worship seemed quite lengthy (two to three hours) and included *two* offerings, one for the church and one for the poor. Inez Dickson made this comment about the latter: "It moved me deeply to see these persons demonstrating their commitment to Christ. So poor themselves, yet they shared in an offering for those who had even less."

Worship was strangely different to the team members, who were seated on wooden benches and listening to voices speaking and singing in Creole. Yet it was also familiar. "Our Christian heritage provided common ground," one said. "As we hummed the tunes of the hymns whose words we could not understand, we surely felt the presence of God." As one after another has observed across the years, "It was a life changing experience."

With four days of strenuous travel and six days of vigorous work, a time for recreation was also built into the schedule. While tourists rarely get to Cap Haitien any more, there are several picturesque and historic sites to visit. Most of the trailblazers visited the Citadelle, the remains of an historic fortress that once defended Cap Haitien. This visit provided an opportunity to learn more about the history of this proud nation that has fiercely defended its independence since 1804.

In spite of the frustration caused by not being able to do all they would have liked to do, each group returned home with a feeling of accomplishment. In spite of the obstacles faced, they knew they had accomplished their mission. They had blazed a trail others could follow.

As the members of Team II departed, they were saddened to leave one of their number behind. Alice White, now a registered nurse, remained to serve an internship at Grace Children's Hospital in Port-au-Prince. In his letter of recommendation for her, Marco Depestre, a prominent leader in the Haitian Methodist Church and one of the directors of the hospital, wrote:

> The Whites are people who want to do personally their part in helping to provide Haitian country people with efficient health assistance. . . . I recommend heartily Mrs. White for the internship which, by informing her on health problems and care in Haiti, will enable her to act efficiently in implementing the vast and generous health program she and her husband have conceived of.

For Alice, it was a rough and lonely time. It was a strange country where the people spoke only Creole and operated their hospital with methods very different from those she had been taught. But she toughed it out, leaving Haiti a month later much better prepared for the role she would play in the future.

With this background and having learned the basics of the Creole language, Alice was now well prepared to guide the medical efforts of the work teams in Haiti. This knowledge and experience, gained at such personal cost, made her the recognized leader of the Haiti Mission. And Alice is the one who has organized, led, inspired, taught, supported, and even "mothered" scores of volunteers in a way that really made a difference.

The Pieces of Eight *shortly after her arrival in Port-au-Prince.*

Top: *Benny Neal, Alberto Dussex, Alice White, and the White airplane in 1981.*
Bottom: *The Tovar Clinic.*

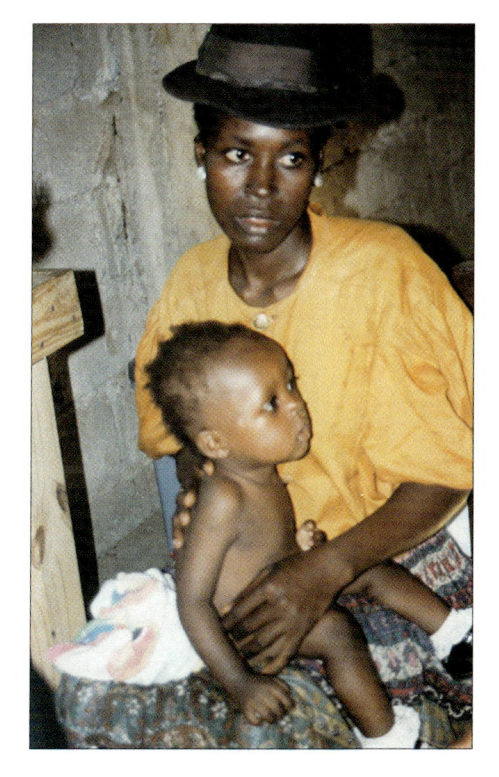

Left: Haitian mother and child await medical care.
Below: Dr. Ginny White Gale and a Haitian child.

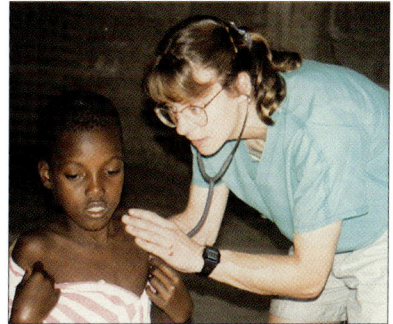

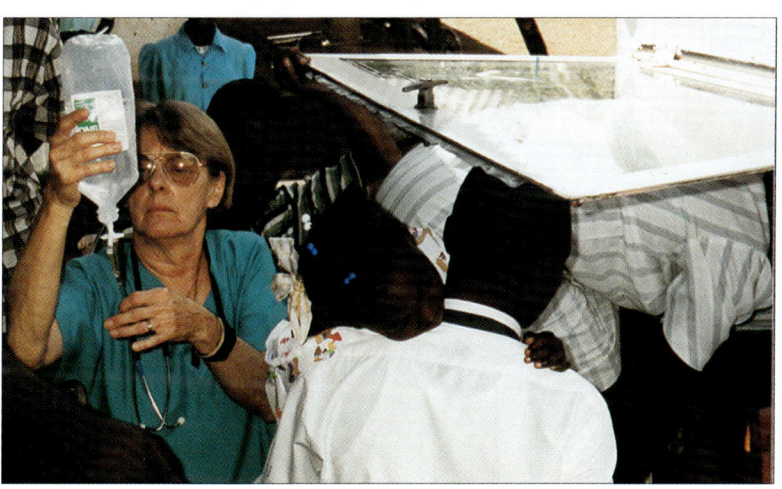

Alice White prepares a child for transfer from Tovar to Hopital Le Bon Samaritain.

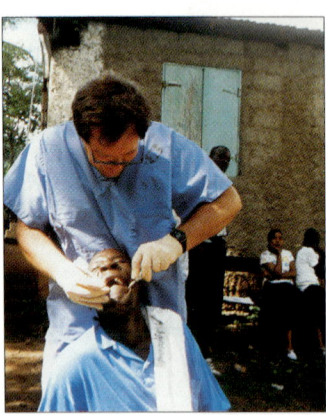

Dr. Bill James in his open-air dental clinic.

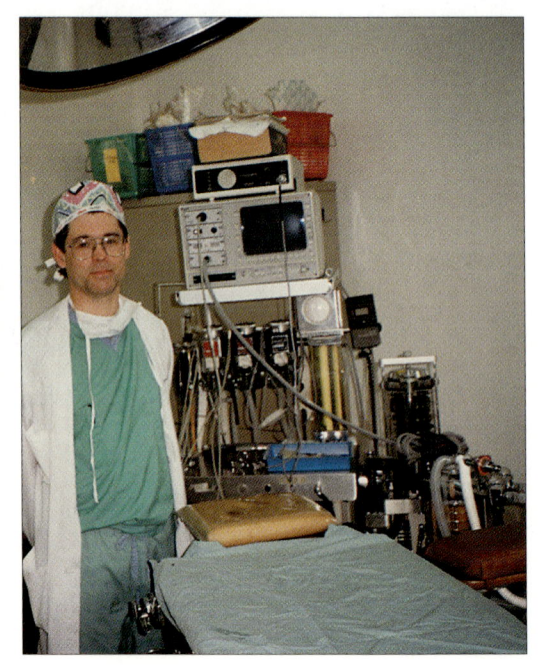

Dr. Mike Barringer at Hopital Le Bon Samaritain.

Left: *Bill White shares plans for construction work at Champin with Luke, the carpenter (left), and Rev. Gesner Paul (center).*
Below: *With the help of Alice White, Dr. Walt Bullington examines eye patients.*

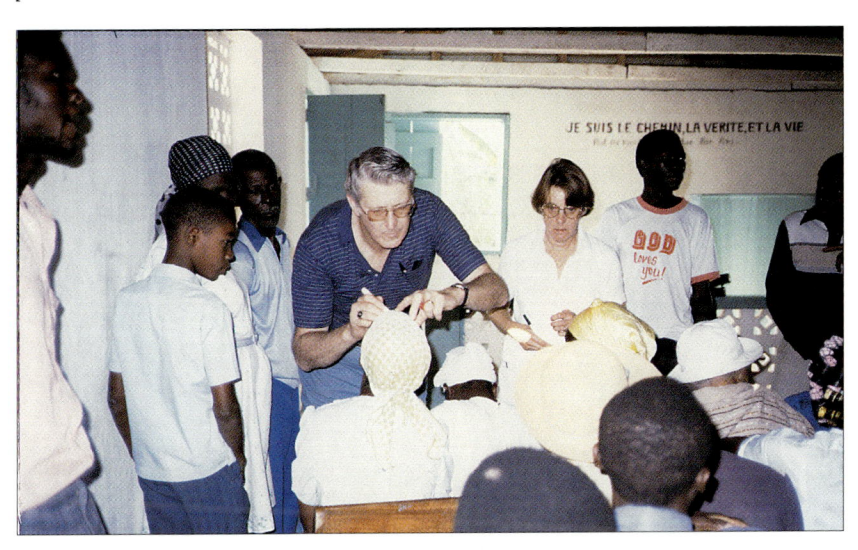

Rev. Gesner Paul walks up the hill to the Latannerie Clinic.

Right: Rev. Larry Wilkinson and his Haitian friend from Dondon, Charlie Martin.
Below: Dr. Patricia Wolff examines mother and child at the Tovar Clinic.

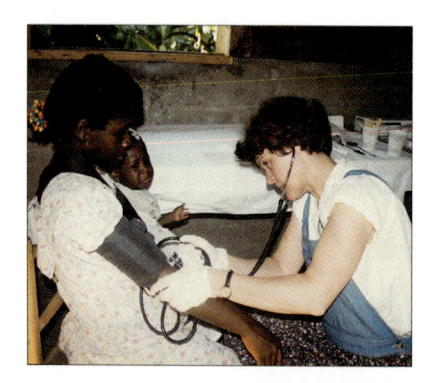

Palm Sunday 1991 dedication service at Champin. This sanctuary was built by Providence Church members with the help of an additional grant from the Western North Carolina Annual Conference.

Above: *Rev. George Freeman talks to children during a worship service at the Cap Haitien Church. Rev. Daniel Bartley acts as interpreter.*
Left: *Anne Bartley and Carolyn Boylan with two Haitian women in the sewing class at Cap Hatien.*
Below: *Several women of Providence Church pack pills for the Haiti Mission.*

Top: *Team II of the 1985 Trailblazers. (Left to right) Bill White, Alice White, Mary Dee Parr, Betty Bowers, Doug Bowers, Shirley Bullington, Wilton Parr, Carolyn Boylan, Walt Bullington, Howard Boylan, and Inez Dickson.*
Bottom: *The JAARS DC-3 and the 1991 medical and construction teams. (Left to right) Louise Maybin, Dick Maybin, Rev. Gesner Paul, copilot Gerry Gardner, mechanic Jim Cartwright, Walt Bullington, Shirley Bullington, Linda Mitchell, (Sue Stephens and Wanda Rogers on boarding ladder), Alice White, Wanda Randolph, Rev. Richard Randolph, Mike Barringer, and pilot Leo Lance.*

CHAPTER 8

The Builders

THE PERIOD BETWEEN 1985 AND 1992 WAS A TIME OF EXPANSION AND GROWTH FOR THE CAP HAITIEN CIRCUIT. "VOLUNTEERS in Mission" groups from Florida, Texas, South Dakota, and North Carolina, working in cooperation with UMCOR and the Haitian Church, provided the money and the labor for several major building projects. In addition to the remodeled building at Dondon, new medical clinics were built at Tovar and Latannerie. New sanctuaries were erected at Dondon, Latannerie, Tovar, Baudin, and Champin. These were the "glory days" for construction work in Haiti.

The Haiti Mission of Providence Church was directly responsible for building the clinics at Dondon and Tovar and the sanctuary building at Champin. As you will see later, they were also indirectly involved in each of the other projects.

While Providence is not generally known as a "blue-collar" church, many of its members do have remarkable amateur abilities in carpentry, plumbing, electrical work, and other related fields. Carpentry was the main skill required, followed closely by a need for helpers willing to do hard labor. And none of this was easy work. As one volunteer observed, "I used muscles I didn't remember having, and every one of them hurt."

With no indoor bathrooms, plumbing skills were not in great demand. Nevertheless, several volunteers were observed doing professional-quality work repairing latrines. A later group even installed a drip irrigation system at the church-owned farm site at Mazaire. When the water finally began to flow, these amateur plumbers celebrated greatly.

While there was no electricity in most areas, amateur electricians got to do some simple wiring in Plain du Nord and Quartier Morin, churches located nearer to Cap Haitien. All in all, quite a few persons were able to use their skills in very practical ways.

Another such practical way involved several women who, encouraged by the Haitian pastor's wife, in 1987 and 1988 used their skills to set up sewing classes. Although these were successful, interest waned after the pastor was transferred to another circuit and the groups were discontinued.

It was a long-range goal of the leaders of the Cap Haitien Circuit to have at Dondon, Tovar, and Latannerie a sanctuary for worship, a weekday school for the children, a medical clinic, and a well with pure drinking water. Even in the face of an overwhelming number of obstacles, that objective had been achieved by 1992. Facilities were in place to enable the church to minister to the physical, mental, and spiritual needs of the people.

The days between 1985 and 1992 were not easy ones for the Providence volunteers. In this poorest and one of the most densely populated nations in the Western Hemisphere, the obstacles to surmount are no less mountainous than the land itself. The builders had "mountains and more mountains" to climb—many roadblocks stood in the way of their success. A more detailed review of those years of service follows.

Paul Bonsall observes as Haitian workers assist Bill White with work on the Tovar Clinic.

The Builders

The first obstacle came shortly after the 1985 teams returned to the United States. While doing some electrical wiring at Plain du Nord, Rev. Holmes fell off a ladder and injured himself seriously. As previously mentioned, after a lengthy time in the hospital, it was determined that it would be best for him to return to England, which he did. Some of his vision for the future of the church was not as clear in the minds of those who carried on. Without his leadership, many of the projects floundered.

The new superintendent of the Cap Haitien Circuit, Rev. Daniel Bartley, arrived in the fall of 1985, young, full of enthusiasm, and just out of seminary. While his later leadership proved to be very effective, his lack of experience added to the confusion of the early days.

Rev. Holmes had specific plans in mind for the clinic at Tovar. However, when the volunteers arrived in January of 1986, they discovered changes had been made. The foundation for the building was at a different place on the site and was much larger. So the teams, and a large number of Haitian workers recruited for the week, were at a standstill. Only a quick redesign of the roof trusses by Bill White and Paul Bonsall, a Charlotte architect and a member of Providence Church,

Trusses for the Tovar Clinic—builders from left to right: Al Rose, Susan Jordan, and Howard Boylan.

saved the day. With their good help, the work was able to proceed on schedule, and before the volunteers had to leave, the roof was essentially in place.

During 1985, a number of other projects were also started on the Cap Haitien Circuit. Under Ed Holmes's direction, Bill White had drawn plans and provided a materials list for three sanctuaries. The design was based on Ed's conception. "I want a church to look like a church." So three churches, using the same distinctive high-pitched roof design, were started. Today they do look very much like churches.

A letter from Rev. Edouard Domond, chairman and superintendent general of Eglisé Methodiste d'Haiti, expressed appreciation for the work Bill had done. "I am pleased to inform you that the work in the three churches is going well, according to the plans submitted to us. We appreciate your coming to Haiti."

Volunteer building teams from other conferences were busy working on these projects. The Reverend Cliff Lamb from Houston, Texas, director of Congregational Development and Church Growth for the Texas Conference, brought teams, as did Don Pike from Arlington, Texas; Hillary Cannon from Roundrock, Texas; and Charles Selph from Winterhaven, Florida. Their work in 1985 and 1986 resulted in the essential completion of sanctuaries at Dondon, Tovar, and Latannerie, as well as a new clinic building at Latannerie.

During January 1986 another team, this one from South Dakota, faced a serious obstacle. Their trip had been scheduled with Ed Holmes, but somehow this was never communicated to Rev. Bartley. While they arrived with the money and the labor to build a sanctuary, they had no plans or materials. Fortunately they were staying at the Beck Hotel, and when their problem became known, Bill White came to their rescue. He "just happened" to have a plan and a material list they could use and knew the place where they could buy materials. The church at Baudin is the beautiful result of this collaboration. Is it any wonder that it looks just like the others? And now you know how the Providence Haiti Mission team was indirectly involved in all of these projects.

More serious political events during January of 1986 created a much larger obstacle. With the dictatorship of Jean-Claude ("Baby Doc") Duvalier rapidly coming apart, anti-government demonstrations flared up across Haiti. A riot in Gonaives effectively closed the only highway, leaving no way for the Haiti Mission team to get back to Port-au-Prince and catch their return flight home. Again the group had to improvise. Rev. Larry Wilkinson later reported these events in his church newsletter.

We determined to look for an alternate route home since our passage to Port-au-Prince and Eastern Airlines was blocked. With the assistance of Dr. Steve Henley, I was able to contact Mission Aviation Fellowship, which usually had a flight into Cap Haitien on Tuesday and Saturday. We learned they were coming into Cap Haitien that day and could fly us to Fort Lauderdale. We were elated to catch their DC-3 for the afternoon flight.

The seriousness of the situation led the Haitian Church and UMCOR to recommend that all volunteer teams postpone their trips. On their way to Haiti, Dr. and Mrs. Walt Bullington were stopped in Miami, and they returned to Charlotte. The trip for Team II was cancelled before its team members left Charlotte.

Duvalier left the country in February, ending a very oppressive dictatorship. Nevertheless, during his rule there had been a certain amount of stability and predictability. The coming of democracy brought with it much uncertainty including invasion, embargo, a takeover by United Nations troops, and many traumatic changes in leadership.

This time of change marked the end of the "glory days" for volunteer teams in Haiti. Since then it has been difficult to schedule work teams, either because of transportation difficulties or due to fear for the safety of the volunteers. Fortunately the work of the Providence Haiti Mission is in the north of Haiti in a relatively isolated area often unaffected by the unrest in other parts of the country. Even with the events of 1986, Larry Wilkinson continued his report this way: "At no time did we feel any hostility from the local Haitians or from the government. Haiti is a nation that needs our prayers and our assistance. I hope we can continue our important ministry in the near future."

Giving further evidence of this continuing commitment to Haiti, he also included these words: "With their own airplane for transportation, Bill and Alice White have remained for a few days to tie up loose ends on the Providence project, and to give further assistance to the team from South Dakota."

This sudden departure of the January team by a different route proved to be a blessing for the future. Since that year, every team from Providence has flown directly to Cap Haitien, avoiding troubled areas and saving valuable time. Traveling can now be done on Saturdays, leaving a full week to work in Haiti. This is especially beneficial to doctors or others who are employed.

For several years all travel was with Mission Aviation Fellowship, a mission airline serving the transportation needs of missionaries in the

Caribbean basin. JAARS, another mission aviation group out of Waxhaw, North Carolina, provided chartered flights for a few groups. Fortunately, Lynx International now provides regular commercial flights from Fort Lauderdale to Cap Haitien.

By now you realize the depth of the commitment Bill and Alice White have made to the Haiti Mission—a commitment that was severely tested in 1986. Shortly after returning from their trip, Bill experienced a serious heart attack, which required an extensive period of recuperation. During that time one of his most serious concerns seemed to be, "Will I be able to fly again?" Later he discovered that he could, but for awhile this was a frightening uncertainty. Not only had he used the airplane in his business, but he had used it also to provide transportation of volunteers and supplies on frequent trips to Haiti.

In the meantime, Alice came to the rescue. With a new commitment on her part, she said, "I will learn to fly!" And she did. Starting at the beginning, she took lessons, soloed, and got her private and instrument licenses in rapid succession. Now the flights to Haiti were guaranteed, and Alice was no longer "just the airplane driver's wife." She could drive the thing herself.

Spurred on with new confidence, a building team was again a part of the Haiti Mission from January 9–18, 1987. With the unrest and uncertainty of the previous year, the Haitians had not accomplished much additional work on the Tovar Clinic. However, the roof was in place and this new team was able to continue work on the inner foundations and walls and pour concrete for part of the floor. They were also able to secure the roof structures, left partially unfinished, on the sanctuaries at Tovar and Latannerie.

Violence surrounding the November 1987 Haitian elections led to a brief postponement of the January 1988 trip. However, after the Whites flew to Cap Haitien and determined that the situation there was stable, the trip was rescheduled for March.

This team built tables and cabinets to finish equipping the Tovar Clinic. It was now ready for full utilization by medical teams, as well as by Haitian doctors and nurses.

A major undertaking for 1988 was the installation of the previously mentioned drip irrigation system at a church-owned farm site at Mazaire. Two wells (with pumps) were bored and a system of underground piping, designed to irrigate a large field drip by drip, was installed. When the team left, it was working.

Unfortunately, maintenance and operation of the system proved to be a problem. A letter from Rev. Daniel Bartley outlined one of the early problems: "It is sad to inform you that one of the parts on the generator has been spoiled or burned. This may happen because the small room was not open

Bill White and Rev. Daniel Bartley congratulate each other when the water begins to flow at Mazaire.

enough that the warmth of the set could come out. Anyhow I send the burned part to you to see if you could get it for us in the United States." While the installation was successful, the system was never used properly, serving to illustrate a common frustration in Haiti. Introducing something new, even something with a potential for great good, does not always work.

Another effort of 1987 and 1988 proved to be helpful but was also short-lived. It was a sewing project instigated by the wife of Rev. Bartley, Anne, who was an accomplished seamstress. Armed with three sewing machines, forty boxes of cloth and other supplies furnished by the women of Providence Church, Carolyn Boylan and Helen Henderson joined Anne in setting up a sewing class. It was hoped that this would not only help some of the women clothe their families but also possibly assist them in finding work if any textile companies set up operations in the area. Unfortunately, the political turmoil prevented that kind of development.

In spite of the long-term outcome, it was an exciting week. Carolyn described it this way:

> We had a room filled with 35–40 women who had heard there was fabric to be had. There are no secrets in Haiti. Each person went home with enough

fabric for a skirt and a blouse. Formal training was difficult because of the excitement of the generous supply of brightly designed cloth. I felt quite inadequate with my limited sewing skills when I saw they could look at a picture and cut the patterns by holding the cloth up to each other for measurements. I'm sure my Home Economics teacher would not have approved, but they could produce a garment with very little fabric. Many are skilled at embroidery and all love to trim their garments with colorful rickrack, buttons, lace, etc. . . . I felt blessed to be allowed simply to be a part of their group and share in the peace and contentment in that small room of women who live in poverty, but know a love for each other and for God.

Carolyn returned in 1988 to work with Anne Bartley, and this time Anne was very much in charge and provided the needed oversight. She gathered a group, including four women from each of the seven churches on the circuit. Some arranged to stay overnight in Cap Haitien, but several had long commutes of an hour or more by "Tap Tap" bus, the only transportation system in Haiti. This week was another success.

But again, as a further illustration of the frustrations of volunteer work in Haiti, Rev. Bartley was assigned to the Petit Goave Circuit in May and replaced in Cap Haitien by the Reverend Gesner Paul. Without Anne Bartley, the sewing class was never the same. Carolyn Boylan still collects fabrics to give to the churchwomen, but no organized program remains.

Rev. Gesner Paul, new superintendent for the circuit, showed an immediate interest in completing the construction work begun by his predecessors. So the January 1989 team was a large one. They focused on building twenty pews, a chancel rail, pulpit, altar, and large cross for the sanctuary at Dondon. They also finished the last section of concrete floor at the Tovar Clinic and repaired several well pumps.

A completely new challenge and opportunity presented itself in 1990. In May of the previous year, the Haitian Methodist Church bought a partially completed building in Champin with the intention of using it as a multipurpose facility for a church, a school, and a clinic. This building was located in a three-hundred-acre urban renewal area on the west side of Cap Haitien, developed under the auspices of the Public Enterprise for Social Housing.

The opportunity to have a Methodist church at this site was too good to pass up, so Rev. Paul and the Haitian leaders appealed to Providence Church to build this new sanctuary. With an estimated price of over $50,000, it was well beyond the budget of the Haiti Mission. But Rev. Larry Wilkinson sought help from Rev. Bob Boggan, director of missions for the Western North Carolina (WNC) Conference. Upon his recommendation, a grant of $15,000 was approved, and with this promise of help, Providence Church committed itself to building the church.

The January 1990 construction team devoted its efforts entirely to this project. Again Bill White drew the plans, this time using a new rigid frame truss design. Lacking workspace on the site, the trusses were built in sections on the grounds of the Beck Hotel. With the masonry work done by Haitian labor, the walls were completed and foundations laid for new portions of the building.

A building team from the WNC Conference was expected to arrive in March to complete the work, but due to a misunderstanding they did not come. So the incompleted trusses were left in storage at the hotel until another Providence team returned in October.

The October group was divided into two teams. The first, assisted by four Haitian carpenters, completed the truss sections; while the second, with the help of six Haitians, prepared scaffolding at the site. A large truck was hired to move the trusses from the Beck Hotel, and both groups combined their efforts to complete the roof. The Haitians were then able to complete the structure and build the chancel and altar furnishings.

When the 1991 team returned on a chartered JAARS flight, the pilot, mechanic, and steward remained in Haiti with the group. They pitched in to help the construction crew build pews and complete the Champin Church. The dedication service for this beautiful facility was held on Palm Sunday 1991 with over three hundred persons present. Providence United Methodist Church could be justly proud. They had helped give birth to a brand new church.

Due to the United Nations embargo imposed on Haiti, the 1992 trip was postponed from January until March. As a result, the group of twenty-three scheduled for January shrunk to eleven in March, and most of these were medical personnel. However, Bill White did work on the well at Latannerie and get it in operation again. While it was not possible to do the work planned on the interior of the sanctuary there, money was left so local workers could complete that task.

Despite all the obstacles faced along the way, the construction work planned for the Cap Haitien Circuit was essentially completed. Clinic buildings were in place at Dondon, Tovar, and Latannerie, and the sanctuaries at Dondon, Tovar, Latannerie, and Baudin were fully in use. The added bonus was the "surprise" new church at Champin.

With adequate facilities in place, future groups could direct their full energies to the medical mission. Since 1992, teams have consisted almost entirely of medical personnel. With that in mind, we now turn our attention from the builders to the doctors.

CHAPTER 9

The Doctors

NUMEROUS DIFFICULTIES STAND IN THE WAY OF TAKING A VOLUNTEER MEDICAL TEAM TO HAITI. AS WITH THE BUILDERS, a lot of these concerns relate to the unrest surrounding political change in the country and to the uncertainty brought about by leadership changes in the church. However, many unique problems face doctors who try to practice modern medicine in a primitive setting.

Why, if it is so hard, do they go? *The Handbook for United Methodist Volunteers in Mission* puts the answer this way: "We go because there is a need for what we do... To do nothing, ignoring those who are asking for help, would indicate that we do not value those who are in need, or those who are trying to help."

With only twelve hospitals and three hundred doctors to serve a population of over six million people, the need is certainly there. So, over the years a large number of persons from various medical fields, obedient to their Christian beliefs and honoring the ethics of their profession, have been a part of the Haiti Mission. A solid core has gone year after year. And their number has increased as word spread from place to place, "If you're interested in helping in Haiti, call Alice White."

Recruiting, organizing, shepherding, and leading a medical group to Haiti is a difficult task at best, and with all the problems uniquely related to Haiti, the outcome often seems doubtful. But it is Alice who always sees that all the people, medicine, and supplies are at the right place at the right time.

Of course, Alice had plenty of help. Two persons became especially able assistants. While not having a medical background, Ann Autrey pitched in and helped in a variety of ways, both before, after, and during the trips. On site, she was excellent with the children and a very helpful assistant to the pediatricians.

Jean Hogsed, like Ann, was a member of Providence Church from Charlotte, North Carolina, and a medical technologist. She participated in five missions during the hard and busy years from 1992 to 1996, getting involved in many ways. Working effectively at the Tovar Clinic, Jean was especially helpful in providing equipment for the laboratory. A special "non-electrical" machine, used to measure red blood count, has been a big asset.

These and many others helped to lighten Alice's load. Yet even with this kind of assistance, it was sometimes questionable whether it could all be pulled together.

THE EARLY YEARS

For the most part, the early years followed the pattern set in 1985. Team I led in January of 1986 with Dr. Fred Miller and his wife Susie returning to do dental work, and Edy was again there to help. The scope of the work was expanded some since Dr. Steve Henley, a short-term missionary from Indiana, was then in the Cap Haitien area and also gave his assistance.

As mentioned earlier, the visit of Team II in 1986 had to be canceled because of the civil disturbances. However a large team was ready to go in 1987. It included Dr. Miller, his wife Susie, Carol Brown, and Edy. The records show they did almost one hundred extractions. After his one-year layoff, Walt Bullington and his wife Shirley returned. By bringing more of his equipment on this trip, Walt was able to treat some of the three hundred patients he saw and also distribute a large number of eyeglasses. However, he continued to be very frustrated. There were no facilities available where he could do some of the surgery he regularly did at home.

Nineteen eighty-eight was a year of expansion. Dr. William James, a periodontist from Charlotte, was looking for some mission involvement, and friends in Charlotte put him in touch with Alice. Upon learning that Fred Miller was not returning, he gladly volunteered his services. This began a longtime relationship with the Haiti Mission, and Bill has been a member of at least one team every year since that time. Not only has he pulled teeth, he also assists in routine examinations and occasionally is called on to suture wounds. During the years when the teams moved from place to place each day, he was in charge of transporting the pharmacy, setting up each morning, and taking down at the end of the day. Bill was also responsible for creating a system for packing certain medicines and vitamins in dose packs. That made it possible to dispense medicines to patients quickly and more efficiently. Now, women from circle groups at Providence package these dose packs ahead of time, consolidating the preparation of medicines for all mission trips.

Another doctor also participated for the first time. Dr. Richard (Dick) Maybin, a general practitioner from Lawndale, North Carolina, had been on mission trips to other parts of the world but was recruited by Rev. Larry Wilkinson. Both his previous experience and a lifetime of practice in the mostly rural areas of upper Cleveland County ideally suited him for the work in Haiti. A willing and tireless worker, he participated in seventeen trips, continuing until shortly before his death in 1999.

Dick's wife Louise always accompanied him. Although not a trained medical worker, she always made a valuable contribution. She was wonderful with the Haitian people, especially the children. It was Louise who conceived the very helpful idea of teaching simple health education lessons to those who were waiting to be seen by a doctor. That is still being done.

One question arose in those early days that had to be answered. To charge or not to charge patients? Both Dr. Miller and Dr. Bullington felt that since they were donating their services, the patient should not have to pay. But the practice in the Methodist Church in Haiti was the opposite. Unless they were totally unable to pay, they were expected to pay a very modest fee.

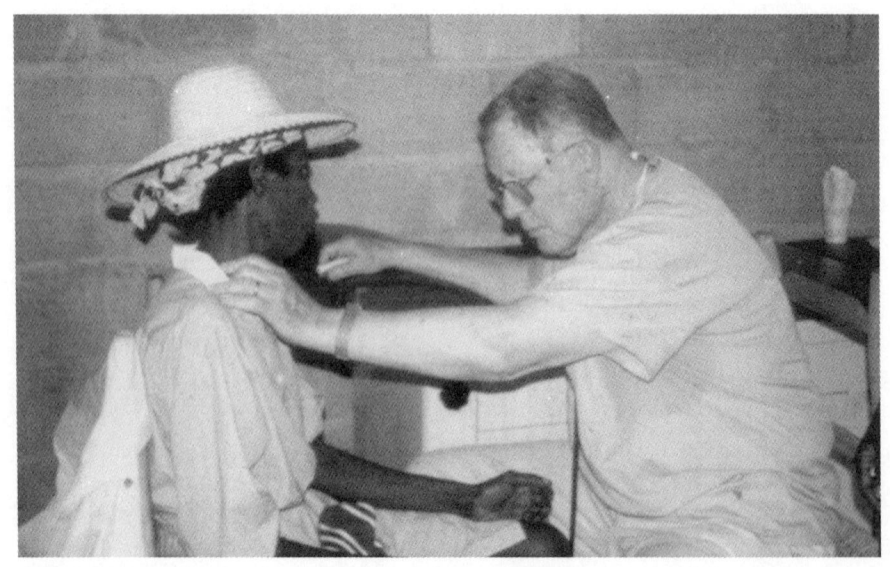

Dr. Richard Maybin at work on one of more than a dozen trips to Haiti.

Louise Maybin in the pharmacy at Tovar.

The subject was discussed with many people. It was found that Dr. Hodges, who ran a charitable Christian hospital in Limbé, always made a small charge, depending on the patient's ability to pay. The church leaders also made a good case for this position, especially Rev. Daniel Bartley. He felt strongly that a fee should be charged, even though it was much less than that of doctors in Cap Haitien, to help teach self-reliance. He did not want to train his people to become dependent on others for their survival.

The Haitian policy prevailed. Today a small fee is charged, although no one is ever turned away for lack of money. The fee income is then applied toward the purchase of additional medicines.

THE SPECIAL YEARS

The years from 1989 to 1992 took on a character of their own. Some even call them the "special years" and for several good reasons. First, there was the fortuitous assignment of Rev. Gesner Paul as the new superintendent of the Cap Haitien Circuit. Not only did he prove to be an excellent leader, but his wife was also a physician. Because she chose not to take a job in Cap Haitien and devoted her time to the church clinics, these clinics were soon opened on a regular basis and became licensed by the government.

Dr. Ginnette Paul, assisted by a Haitian nurse, Maryse Isidore, and others, did very effective work there. When the Haiti Mission volunteers came, it was much easier for them to set up to do their work. They also knew that when they returned home, someone would be around to see patients on a year-round basis. So, the mission teams continued to come, and the Haiti Mission also began to help fund and ship medicines to the clinics on a year-round basis.

While 1989 and 1990 continued to be frustrating years for Dr. Bullington, he and his wife Shirley still came each year. He discussed doing surgery in Limbé with Dr. Hodges, the owner of Hopital Le Bon Samaritain. However, the hospital had a backlog of patients with more critical needs, so there never was any space for him to do eye surgery. But, as I said, these were special years, and finally in 1991 a special breakthrough came. When Dr. Hollis Clark opened the Baptist Eye Center in Cap Haitien, he invited Walt to do cataract surgery there. This gave him the ability to treat some of the patients he had never been able to help, and he was overjoyed. Both he and Shirley described that January week as "the best week in their life."

Dr. Mike Barringer, a surgeon from Shelby, North Carolina, was also introduced to Haiti in 1991. Carl Poole, from Cleveland County, North Carolina, and a member of one of the building teams, was a patient of Mike's. One day he said, "Mike, why don't you come to Haiti?" That proved to be a very worthwhile conversation. In 1991 Mike came to the Hopital Le Bon Samaritain to help with their large backlog of surgical cases. This marked the beginning of a very special relationship between Mike and the hospital. The surgical aspects of the Haiti Mission are so important they will be covered separately in the next chapter.

For a while it seemed that only good things would occur, and the special years would go on and on. Unfortunately, it never seems to work out that way, certainly not in Haiti. In September of 1991 President Aristide was deposed in a military coup and fled the country. The reaction to the overthrow of a duly elected democratic official was swift. Both the Organization of American States (OAS) and the United States declared an economic embargo of Haiti, hoping thereby to force the return of Aristide to power. The embargo had little effect on the military dictatorship, but threw the country into turmoil.

The 1992 Haiti Mission trip was scheduled for January. However, as there was no gasoline and very little food in Cap Haitien and the political situation was unfavorable, the trip was postponed. Nevertheless, in February Bill and Alice flew to Cap Haitien with their airplane loaded with food and medicine and spent several days visiting friends. Other than a very dismal scene, worse because of the embargo, they saw nothing to prevent them from going back for a regular visit.

So, with eleven of the twenty-three persons that had been scheduled for the January trip, a team finally arrived in Haiti on March 13. Alice described the visit this way:

Because the medical team was short-staffed, the job of seeing the volume of patients who needed medical attention was difficult. Several of the Haitians were pressed into service to do additional tasks. One of the interpreters helped do vital signs, and another helped count pills and explain dosages. The team worked at two clinics, Tovar and Latannerie. Each day began with a prayer in the church, where everyone waited patiently to be seen, and though the days were long, no one complained, and everyone was seen.

Before we left, Rev. Gesner Paul thanked us for coming, *not only in the good times, but in the bad times as well.* He told us that we were the

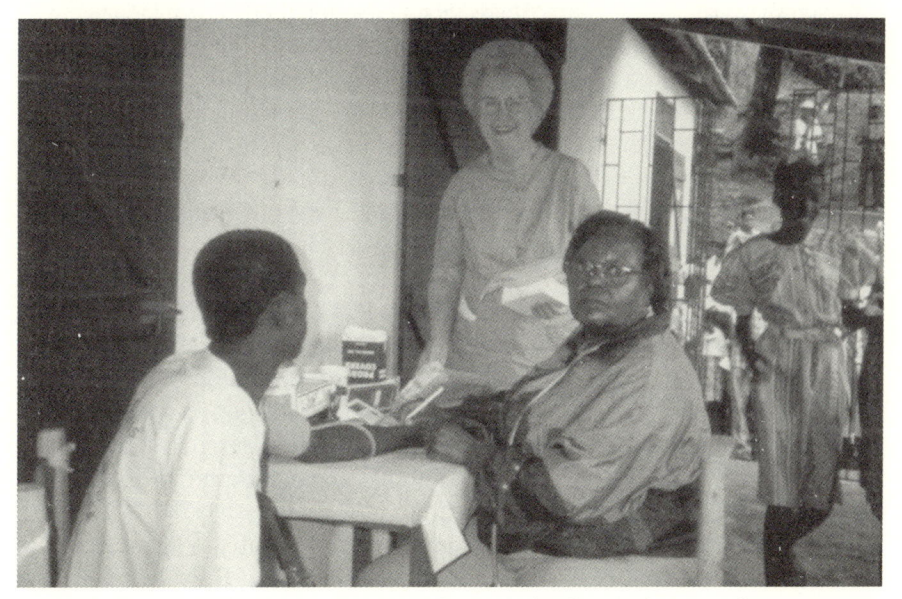

Mary Coleman looks on as Marian Thomas checks vital signs of a patient at the Latannerie Clinic.

only Methodist team to come to Cap Haitien since the coup, and that the people feel abandoned, but we have given them hope. Our being here showed that we cared about them.

To add to these unfortunate circumstances, it was announced that Rev. Paul and his wife Ginnette were being transferred to another circuit. So after three years of growth and hope, the clinics again had no physician, and the Haiti Mission no longer had the leadership of this special couple.

THE HARD YEARS

The aura around the special years quickly faded as the "hard years" of 1992–1994 began. The situation can best be portrayed in the words Alice White used to describe what happened:

> The January 1993 mission was an all-medical project . . . we worked in three villages, two days at Tovar, one at Dondon, and two days at Latannerie. Our doctors saw 779 patients and the dentist 148. In all, 592 teeth were pulled.

> There is no health care for the poor, and 99 percent of the population is poor. Because of the embargo there are no jobs, and therefore no income, so most Haitians cannot go to a doctor. . . . Generally, the condition of those who came to our clinics was worse than in past visits, with more malnutrition, infections, parasites, and G.I. disorders usually from bad water and little food.

> The Haiti Mission finds itself in an unexpected role; the sole source of health care for many people.

Another team returned in September 1993 and the medical team, headed by Dr. Richard Maybin, again visited the same three clinics. The final patient count was 680, and on Friday three doctors saw 188 persons—a record for a single day. The patient load had increased, and the people were generally sicker. The report for that trip reminded all that two of these clinic buildings, Dondon and Tovar, were built by Providence United Methodist Church building teams.

Rev. Lebrun Corsaire, the new superintendent of the Cap Haitien Circuit appointed in 1992, was very supportive of the Haiti Mission. In her report Alice commended him, his wife, and the Haitian participants, without whom the work would not happen.

Rev. Corsaire and his wife Margaret have been outstanding in their support of this program. They and the others on the Haitian team consisting of a nurse, a part-time doctor, the registrar, and several interpreters, are enormously important to the mission. Also, several members of local churches volunteer their services whenever we are there. Over the years, we have all become closer as the struggle continues to worsen.

Several of the interpreters were schoolboys when we first came. By working with another interpreter and one of the doctors, they have improved their language skills enough to work on the team, and they are also learning to take vital signs, work in the pharmacy, and assist in giving vaccinations.

The January 1994 team added Baudin to the list of places visited. The total number of patients seen soared to 1,111, with a greater number seriously ill. The record of 188 patients seen in a day at Latannerie the previous year was broken on each of these five days. On Friday, they treated 247 patients and one dog, as Dr. Joe Minus reported. Dr. Minus always had trouble sleeping, usually he said because of barking dogs. So, when one patient approached him, along with a dog that would not leave her side, he endured it. However, he felt that since he had recommended flea powder and dog biscuits for it, the dog needed to be recorded in the daily record.

As the effects of the embargo increased dramatically, Alice observed:

> In many cases it can be proved that malnutrition and deaths in children are caused by the embargo. The caregiver has no job, and therefore no money for food or care. In other cases the effects are less direct, but usually traceable to the debilitated and depressed condition of Haiti, where medical facilities are closed and other humanitarian agencies lack the resources to give out food or care. Families move in together in crowded and unhealthy living conditions. In many cases some are even moved out into the streets.

With the fuel shortage, travel in the country was nearly impossible. But the Haitian Church members proved their love for the work of the Haiti Mission. Long before a team arrived, they began to store fuel for its use even though it was very expensive. This made it possible for the team to function normally, moving both medical and surgical teams from one place to another.

After the 1994 team returned home, Alice chose to stay an additional two weeks at the Hopital Le Bon Samaritain in Limbé to lend a hand.

This also served to give her a broader view of the effects of the embargo. Upon her return she reflected upon conditions she observed.

> Undeniably, the embargo has destroyed Haiti's economy and social structure. It has caused a great increase in infant mortality, malnutrition and human suffering, from lack of food and medical care. There is no justification for such a heartless policy.
>
> Very few people are employed, and there is almost no commerce. Most businesses have closed, and in many cases have moved to other countries never to return, because of sanctions against imported and exported goods. Most hotels are closed. There are no tourists, and few traveling for business reasons. There is no power in the cities, and very little telephone service. Roads are in total disrepair and garbage is left piled in the streets.
>
> Commodities such as gasoline are prohibited but, when available, gas costs fifteen dollars a gallon or more. Without jobs or income, most Haitians cannot afford to pay the increased fares to ride the "tap-taps" to market, so they cannot sell their produce and buy food for their families.

The fall mission trip, scheduled for October, had to be canceled due to the return of Aristide and the U.S. invasion of Haiti. Travel into Haiti was almost totally restricted. No commercial carriers could enter the country, and only Missionary Flights International (MFI), a nonprofit missionary service courier was flying. Even this was infrequent and quite uncertain.

A license for any flight had to be issued by the U.S. Treasury Department and the United Nations, and this usually took weeks. But, determined not to desert their friends in Haiti, Alice and Bill pulled out all stops and finally received a license to fly their small airplane into Cap Haitien. Let Alice tell the rest of her story.

> This brought the number of airplanes granted permission to land in Haiti at that time to two (MFI's and the Whites). At the end, the schedules of the two merged, and arrangements were made to fly our small plane to Florida and load its cargo in the DC-3 and hitch a ride. On November 8, the day after the U.S. military opened the Cap Haitien airport, MFI landed.
>
> We recruited a team, consisting of our interpreters and two Haitian doctors. In the past the interpreters had been taught certain clinical skills, such as taking vital signs and working in the pharmacy. And so,

this almost all-Haitian team in five clinic days saw 726 patients. In keeping with our history, and strong conviction that in times of greatest difficulty the need for help is greatest, we did not have to cancel our trip.

THE BUSY YEARS

With the embargo lifted, and U.N. International Police Monitors (United Nations Police Moniteurs Internationale) performing a peace-keeping role in the country, a full medical team was able to return in January of 1995. In the aftermath of suffering brought on by the embargo, the two years from January 1995 to January 1997 proved to be very busy years. During this twenty-four-month period, eight separate medical teams made the trip to Haiti.

The January group faced a new challenge when they found that fifty-eight of the U.N. International Police Monitors were barracked at the Beck Hotel. They were mostly young recruits from the Caribbean. Alice described this week as:

> . . . a broadening experience in many ways. A large television set on the porch outside our rooms played 24 hours a day at the top of the volume register. Our team, totally spent from long days with patients, did not get much sleep.
>
> One day our team was unable to travel to the clinic because torrential rains had washed out the mountain road. So, as a gesture of peace and good will, our doctors volunteered to have sick bay for the troops. Interestingly enough, all fifty-eight came. According to their medic, it had been difficult to get medicine for them. While they were greatly appreciative and relations improved, it did not get much quieter at night.

These were frustrating times in many ways since the Haiti Mission had become the sole health provider for a large segment of Haiti's poor. In one week during January three doctors saw 1,300 patients, pulled 200 teeth, and vaccinated 234 children for measles.

It was becoming obvious that some changes needed to be made so that more people could be treated. So the October team, consisting entirely of registered nurses working with Haitian help, chose to work a full week at the Latannerie Clinic. They hoped in this way they would be able to see all the people who were ill. Quite the opposite happened. As word spread, more and more came each day—175, 205, 218, 245, and on

Friday 250. What they learned was, "With millions of poor in Haiti, the longer we stay, the more will come."

As a result of this experiment, it was decided to recruit two teams for January 1996. It was the largest group ever, with nine medical doctors and a periodontist. They divided their efforts with one team spending a full week at Tovar. The intention was that the other would spend its week at Latannerie, except for one day at Dondon. That plan was followed with one exception. A roadblock prevented the second team from going to Latannerie on Friday.

> Some team members, coming to Latannerie from Hopital Le Bon Samaritain Thursday afternoon to help take the medical team back, came to a roadblock. It was a statement of protest, either by a political faction or one side of a land dispute, and no one was able to pass. Using good judgment, our team members went to the airport and reported the incident to the U.N. Commanding Officer. He mustered several truckloads of Pakistani peacekeepers, who went to the scene and cleared the road. This protest was not directed toward us; there was no intent to harm anyone, and several photos recorded the event.
>
> However, because of the disturbance the clinic visit on Friday was cancelled. Two members of the team, and Rev. Corsaire, did go to the clinic and explained to the waiting crowd why the doctors would not be there. It was also announced that a Haitian doctor and nurse would be at the clinic for three days the following week. This was paid for by the Haiti Mission so that those waiting would not go away without help, and that hopefully each would get the medical care they needed.

In spite of the roadblock, 1,874 patients were seen during the two-week period. The Haitian team, returning the next week, saw an additional 300 to 400 people.

It was an especially memorable trip for Dr. Sam Joyner and Bill White, who handled their own serious chest pains during the return trip with all the Nitrostat they could find. Sam had coronary bypass surgery the next week; Bill had the same a few months later.

Another effort to enlarge the scope of the mission occurred in May. Working with Jean Broyles from Roanoke, Virginia, Alice White helped arrange for a volunteer group from that area to visit the clinics. A group of thirteen, comprised of doctors, nurses, and support personnel, made up their team. Alice and Dee Brooks went along to act as a liaison between the Roanoke team and the Haitian Church. The Roanoke report indicated that:

The physicians examined and treated approximately 1,100 patients and prescriptions were filled for most of the patients for vitamins, iron, worm medicine, antibiotics, Tylenol, ibuprofen, and other common drugs. Many received reading glasses supplied by the Roanoke Lion's Eyeglass Recycling Center. . . . The children especially are malnourished and anemic, and most have intestinal parasites and scabies. . . . There are many we are sure will die before the next team comes in January.

With the need so great, some extra money was found so that an additional team could make an unscheduled October visit. Dr. Maybin, Dr. Kevin Rossiter from Columbia, Maryland, and Dr. Matthew Goldsmith from St. Louis, Missouri, were the doctors in the group. Three new team members were also added who have continued to be a valuable asset for the Haiti Mission: Marsha Clark from Lawndale, North Carolina, who came along to assist Dr. Maybin; Mrs. Jerre Boren, R.N., from Elkin, North Carolina, a pharmacology teacher; and Gail Rogers, R.N., from Asheville, North Carolina, an optometry nurse. Since this marked the first involvement of Rev. David Bidnell, the newly assigned superintendent of the circuit, Bernard Gilles, a Haitian interpreter, handled most of the local details.

Again, for January of 1997 two medical teams were recruited. The first spent five days at Tovar seeing one thousand patients. The second got to spend only four days at Latannerie. (This time a nationwide protest strike against the government closed the road.) Still, nine hundred patients were seen.

THE CRISIS YEARS

Then came the crisis. A government policy had been adopted providing that no team from outside the country could practice medicine except in a full-time licensed clinic. This was a serious obstacle for the Haiti Mission. Not since Rev. Paul and his wife Ginnette had left in 1992 had any of the clinics on the Cap Haitien Circuit been operated on a full-time basis, and consequently none were eligible for a license.

This policy had been known for some time, and attempts were under way to find a way to obtain a license for the clinic at Tovar. During this time, the Haiti Mission was given special permission to continue with the October visit as well as the one for January 1997. Then, however, the grace period came to an end. The minister of health canceled the second visit of the Roanoke, Virginia, team scheduled for May of 1997. This was indeed a devastating blow. Unless some clinic could become licensed, no Haiti Mission group could return to the Cap Haitien Circuit.

I am told that the Chinese word for crisis includes two meanings: danger and opportunity. Obviously there was the real danger that the whole project might have to come to an end. Fortunately opportunity was present as well. An appeal had been made to the minister of health to allow the Haiti Mission to continue as before but to no avail. However, opportunity presented itself in the form of Fiona Bidnell, wife of the Reverend Bidnell, new superintendent of the Cap Haitien Circuit. The couple had come to Haiti from England where David completed his theology work at the University of Manchester and Fiona received her degree in electrical engineering. She had also honed her managerial skills with several years of work experience. Fortunately for the medical work in the Cap Haitien area, she showed a keen interest in the clinics. And it was Fiona who took the lead in developing a proposal for the licensing of the Tovar Clinic.

Historically the operation of the clinics came under the direction of the pastor. We remember this from the days of Rev. Ed Holmes. However, over the years a change was made. In order to relieve the pastor from this responsibility and to enable the church to have a coordinated approach, a central office for the Coordination of Development (COD) was formed in Port-au-Prince. Their main activities involved literacy, rural economy, and community health. With this joint effort, funding could be obtained from non-governmental organizations, while local churches also could still request direct funding for special projects. Mme. Inette Durandis became the general director of COD, with Ichmide Morisset serving under her as the director of development for the Cap Haitien Circuit.

Fiona Bidnell worked diligently with these Haitian leaders to prepare a detailed proposal for the full-time operation of the Tovar Clinic. Then in May of 1997, Alice and Bill flew to Haiti and joined Fiona as she, Mme. Durandis, and Ichmide Morisset presented their joint proposal to Dr. Jean Myrtho Julien, minister of health for the north of Haiti. After an on-site inspection on May 20, he approved the recommendation, which also included an estimate of the cost of repairs that needed to be made to the building.

With the Haiti Mission providing much of the funding, the work got under way to prepare Tovar to become a facility licensed by the Haitian government. This would further enable them to buy medicine at the World Health Organization (WHO) pharmacy in Cap Haitien at a very low price. The Haiti Mission also provided other supplies, equipment, and certain medicine not available from WHO.

The grand day finally arrived. In early December of 1997, the Tovar Clinic opened as a full-time, fully staffed community health center. A Haitian doctor and a lab technician now come to the clinic twice a week.

Two auxiliary nurses, a pharmacist, two administrators, a watchman, and a cleaner are there five days a week. Fortunately one of the administrators is Fiona Bidnell. Her business background has proved to be an invaluable asset.

The first full year was indeed a good one. The final report indicated that 6,275 persons passed through the clinic, about 45 percent of them children. This was almost three times the volume possible prior to the full-time operation. In addition, Haiti Mission teams came three times that year (in January, May, and October) to work side by side with the Haitian staff to augment the level of services which could be provided. And, upon their return home, volunteers now have the satisfaction of knowing that patients will continue to receive help on a year-round basis.

THE FUTURE

In Haiti when you have climbed one mountain, you can usually expect to climb another one soon. And so it is. In early 1999 David and Fiona Bidnell announced their return to England. A new superintendent will be assigned to the Cap Haitien Circuit. Another crisis. Who will replace Fiona as the manager of the clinic? What will happen to the proposal she was preparing for the reopening of the clinic at Latannerie? Will the Tovar Clinic continue to operate? Can the Haiti Mission continue?

Who knows? The future is always uncertain—a mixture of doubt, guesswork, and hope. And you can be certain this is true in Haiti. But hopefully every crisis also contains opportunity. I'm betting on that.

Can the amazing skill of Alice White keep medical teams coming to Haiti? With all I know, I'm betting on that, too. Doctor Raymond Ford from Charlottesville, Virginia, spoke of her skills in this way: "I stand in awe of what you have accomplished, Alice. I never did know a broody hen that could cover and care for as many eggs as you do!"

With Alice and Bill, and a loyal group from Providence Church totally committed to the Haiti Mission, I have confidence that it will continue. With all the prayers for help rising on behalf of the poor of Haiti, I have no doubt that new answers will be ready for the difficult questions that lie ahead.

Chapter 10

The Surgeons

THIS FASCINATING STORY OF THE SURGEONS IS PRIMARILY ABOUT TWO MEN, DR. WALTER G. BULLINGTON AND DR. Michael L. Barringer. Walt was a Charlotte ophthalmologist and a long-time member of Providence United Methodist Church. His story is significant but necessarily short. Mike is a young surgeon from Shelby, North Carolina, a member of Aldersgate United Methodist Church, and has a constantly growing commitment. His story gets longer with each passing year. The work of these two, and others inspired by them, has added another much-needed dimension to the Haiti Mission.

From the beginning, Dr. Bullington realized that many of the patients he was seeing needed to have some form of eye surgery. Unfortunately, there was no place for him to do what he did so easily in the United States. In spite of this unmet need, Walt continued to come to Haiti each year, doing eye exams, giving medicines to a few, and delivering eyeglasses to many.

Each visit included time spent trying to locate a suitable place to do surgery. On one trip he drove to Pignon to check out a hospital run by a Haitian doctor with a medical degree from the United States. He was welcome, but getting to such a remote area, two hours out of Cap Haitien, just was not practical.

The Christian hospital at Limbé also offered a possibility. But most of the three hundred surgery cases on backlog were considered more critical than were his eye patients. He could do surgery there, but not now.

Then Walt met Dr. Hollis Clark. Dr. Clark was hoping to open an eye center at the Baptist Mission in Cap Haitien. And yes, he would be happy for Walt to help, but he wasn't sure when the clinic would be ready. So

Walt, and his wife Shirley, put aside their frustrations and continued to do what they could.

They first came to Haiti in 1985 and returned in 1987, 1988, 1989, and 1990. Then, finally, in late 1990 the long-awaited letter arrived. The Baptist Eye Center was open, and Dr. Clark invited Walt, when he came in January, to help with cataract surgery. Without hesitation, Walt accepted.

Civil disorder in Cap Haitien delayed the January trip, but in February his long-awaited dream came true. This time Walt felt he really helped, and in a way for which he was best suited. When he and Shirley returned home, they reported that this was the best week of their lives. And why not? Many, who had been blind, now could see.

Walt and Shirley were able to return to the Eye Center in 1992 and 1993. Unfortunately, Walt's health did not permit them to continue beyond that time. After a lingering illness, he died in 1998. Out of respect for his life and his work in Haiti, a permanent endowment fund was established in his memory. The "Bullington Fund" will provide income that will help the Haiti Mission continue its ministry of healing for many years to come.

Nineteen ninety-one was also the year that Dr. Mike Barringer volunteered for the Haiti Mission and spent his first week tackling the large backlog of surgery cases at Hopital Le Bon Samaritain in Limbé. Dr. William H. Hodges, an American doctor with a strong missionary commitment, had operated this private Christian hospital, affiliated with the American Baptist Convention, since 1958. Under his direction the hospital evolved from a small clinic into a large primary health care center, serving an area of the country with a mostly rural population of 1.2 million people.

With help from the Willow Creek Community Church in Michigan, a two-room surgical suite was added to the hospital in 1988. A retired surgeon, and one or two part-time persons, used the facility but could not come close to keeping up with the huge need for surgery. The hospital was conveniently located about forty-five minutes from Cap Haitien and about the same distance from Tovar, so in 1989 Alice paid a visit to Dr. Hodges to see if anything could be done to help. With his encouragement, she and Dr. James Detorre, an orthopedic surgeon from Hilton Head, South Carolina, returned in January and made arrangements for him to lead a team that would come to Hopital Le Bon Samaritain in January of 1991. When these plans were finalized, the team was recruited.

Unfortunately when the January civil disturbance in Cap Haitien forced a change in dates, Dr. Detorre was unable to adjust his schedule

Alice White, with Dr. William Hodges, the head of Hopital Le Bon Samaritain on her right, and Dr. Margie Borrerro on her left.

and had to cancel. This left Mike Barringer as the sole surgeon, and he brought along Wanda Rogers, his regular scrub nurse in Shelby. Shirley Bullington, Walt's wife, coordinated the work of both surgical teams—at Limbé and at the Baptist Eye Center—and did anesthesia for Mike. Sue Stephens rounded out the group, acting as circulating nurse.

No written records are available to provide details of this first visit, but both Mike and Wanda remember this as a productive and satisfying time. In a letter to Alice and Bill, Wanda described her feelings this way: "I want to let you know how grateful I am . . . missionary work has been a dream of mine for a long time and the Haiti Mission trip was the most meaningful experience of my life. . . . It was great to be able to help other people who are really in need . . . my life was really blessed."

A later summary of a similar one-week visit by Mike gives us a good idea of the kinds of surgical procedures involved.

> . . . we performed seven hysterectomies, five adult hernia repairs, one infant hernia repair, one hydrocelectomy, two vagotomies and antrectomies, one mastectomy, one C-section, three breast biopsies, one skin graft, repair of a tracheoesophageal fistula, one thyroidectomy, and several other minor procedures.

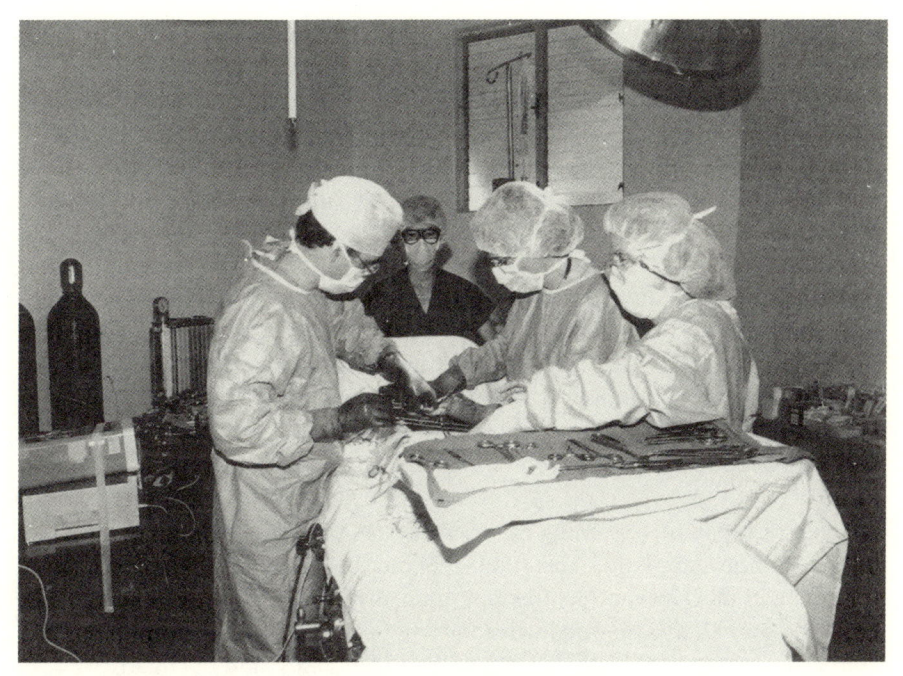

Surgical team at Hopital Le Bon Samaritain—left to right: Dr. Barringer, Shirley Bullington, Sue Stephens, and Wanda Rogers.

Mike developed an instant love for the work in Haiti. First he returned each year, then twice a year, and then for two weeks twice a year. Now he makes two trips a year, spending six weeks each time. His commitment has been a blessing for the Haiti Mission and for a large number of people who have been healed through his surgery. Mike says he feels called to this mission, and the story of his recruitment bears that out.

Carl Poole, from Shelby and a member of the 1989 building team, heard several discussions about the need for a surgeon. He also happened to be a patient of Dr. Barringer. Knowing Mike only as his doctor, he was reluctant to approach him. But finally, while in his office for treatment, he just blurted it out. "Why don't you come to Haiti and help?"

What Carl did not know was that Mike had been to Haiti once, serving two weeks of his surgical residency in Port-au-Prince, and had an unspoken desire to return. Thus it did not take much persuasion. After consulting with Dr. Maybin, a Cleveland County medical colleague, and talking with Bill and Alice White, he agreed to be a part of the 1991 team.

Did this "just happen?" You are entitled to your own opinion, but Mike's participation in the Haiti Mission certainly has proved to be a true calling in the best sense of the word. A full evaluation of the effects of his contribution will have to wait until some time in the future, but it is important that we look now at what he has already done.

First, the amount of surgery Mike does is phenomenal. His February report in 1997 said this, "Since 1991 I have spent a total of 18 weeks at Hopital Le Bon Samaritain, performing well over 500 operations."

During this period he was spending only one or two weeks on each trip to the country. Now that he is in Haiti for two six-week visits each year and also is recruiting others to go, the number of procedures has increased dramatically. His report for January-February 1999 shows that Mike performed 179 procedures and several members of the team also worked in the maternity, medical, and pediatric areas of the hospital. Do not think of these numbers as mere statistics. Think what would have happened to hundreds of Haitians if Mike had not been there to help.

Mike especially likes to remember one of these people:

> One of my most rewarding experiences was the procedure performed on Sadrac Abraham. This nine-year-old boy was born without a connection between his rectum and his anus. He lived with a colostomy all this time and was somewhat of an outcast. In October we did an operation to pull his rectum down to his anus and in January we closed his colostomy. While we were there Sadrac began having normal bowel movements.
>
> Before we arrived, Sadrac told Joanna Hodges he was looking forward to his operation, because if it went well he would be a *real boy*. Thanks to the effort of your mission Sadrac now is a *real boy* and does not have to suffer the severe stigma attached to people in Haiti who have colostomies.

While Dr. Barringer is the surgical team leader, he is by no means the only surgeon to volunteer for the Haiti Mission. Ginny White Gale, daughter of Bill and Alice White (the one child who did *not* get to help sail the *Pieces of Eight* to Haiti), participated in several missions and twice while doing her surgical residency. Dr. Ben Timmons, plastic surgeon from Gastonia, North Carolina, was extremely helpful with general surgery but also operated on four children with cleft palates. He reported, "It's satisfying to know that I got to help people who would not get this kind of help normally."

Other volunteer surgeons included Larry Whitten, John Kelly, Robert Ledbetter, Philip Klim, Deysey Klein, and Katie Minnick. With Mike now responsible for the year-round scheduling at Hopital Le Bon Samaritain, the list continues to grow.

In addition to performing operations, Mike has been able to direct a large amount of equipment and supplies to Hopital Le Bon Samaritain. With his help, it became a sister hospital to Cleveland Memorial Hospital in Shelby, an affiliate of the Carolinas Medical Center in Charlotte. This relationship has *not* provided financial help but has allowed him access to older equipment, replaced by his hospital, which was either donated or purchased at a good price. Supplies are also available at a greatly reduced price, and some are donated to the mission. A 1994 report outlined equipment added to the hospital up to that time:

> . . . the hospital has been provided newer EKG and X-ray machines as well as an automatic film processor; a chemistry unit; an isolette; up to date monitors which provide electrocardiogram, blood pressure and oxygen saturation measurements; two excellent cautery units; cystoscopy equipment; a microscope; a small steam sterilizer; a more advanced anesthesia machine and equipment; and on our last trip an ultrasound unit, that will be of tremendous value in their obstetrical work. In addition to these specific pieces of equipment we have shipped tens of thousands of dollars in the form of support equipment such as suture, drapes, gowns, tubing, drugs, and other supplies.

These improvements would not have been possible without Mike's genuine interest, and his commitment continues to grow. When he found that one week once a year was not satisfactory, he began going two weeks at a time saying, "One week is not enough to get to know the place." Before long he was going for two weeks at a time and then two weeks twice a year.

Feeling the need to make a deeper commitment, he made a new resolve in 1997. "I'll tithe my time to Haiti." After discussing this with the other four surgeons in his Shelby clinic, they made a decision that allowed him even more involvement. The partners agreed that he could take three months each year for his Haiti work. Now Mike is there for six weeks in January/February and six weeks in September/October.

While part of this time is considered vacation, much is not, and his participation is a genuine gift of time and money. Mike knows this. "If you give only your time," he says, "it's really no sacrifice."

Year after year he has returned to Haiti, both in the best of times and in the worst of times. This commitment has earned him the complete respect of the hospital staff at Hopital Le Bon Samaritain. Their appreciation was expressed in these words, "You came when no one else did. You stayed when everyone else left."

With a strong sense that what he is doing is being done for God, Mike feels deeply that God will provide whatever is needed to get the work done in Haiti. New duties are a constant test of that faith. With the death of Dr. Hodges in 1995, Mike became a member of the Hospital Board. Just prior to that time the Hopital Le Bon Samaritain (HBS) Foundation was established to take over in case of Dr. Hodges's death. A similar foundation was also set up in Florida to receive U.S. donations on behalf of the hospital. This is the foundation to which Mike has been named a member.

While Hopital Le Bon Samaritain is no longer affiliated with the American Baptist Convention, it still receives much help from its many supporters in the United States. These contributions provide about one-third of the needs of a six-hundred-thousand-dollar annual budget. The rest has to come from fees, necessarily small, and much of that comes from surgery patients. Even when Mike says that a hernia operation costs a patient only forty U.S. dollars, you can see that his work makes an important contribution to the hospital.

Still, Mike's responsibility continues to grow. Not only is he a member of the Hospital Board, but he has also agreed to be in charge of surgery. In addition to his work with the Haiti Mission, it is his duty to recruit and schedule surgeons who come at other times during the year. With Mike's help, volunteer surgeons at Hopital Le Bon Samaritain now work a total of about six months out of each year.

It is no wonder that Emily Hodges, Dr. Hodges's daughter-in-law, recently said about Mike Barringer, "He is just like one of our family." Though he is considered part of the "Hodges Family," he remains an indispensable part of the "Haiti Mission" family. With his help, the Hopital Le Bon Samaritain has become an invaluable ally of the Haiti Mission outreach.

Before this relationship existed, there was no help for critically ill patients who came to Tovar or one of the other clinics. Now, when it is deemed advisable, patients may be referred, or sent, or taken from one of the clinics to Hopital Le Bon Samaritain, knowing they will be admitted and, if possible, receive the help they need.

In 1997 an eighteen-year-old female came to the clinic with keloids (growths) on her earlobes the size of grapefruits, which hung almost to her shoulders. She was sent to see Mike at Hopital Le Bon Samaritain on Wednesday. On Friday, she returned to the clinic, proudly showing the results of her successful surgery.

Many others, not needing surgery but in desperate need of hospital care, can be referred to Hopital Le Bon Samaritain as well. The following is a case in point.

At Tovar on Monday there was a little girl, about two years old, who was so badly dehydrated that the pediatrician said that if she didn't have intravenous fluids she would probably be dead in a day. It was decided that the minister and Bill White would take the child and her grandmother to Limbé, some forty miles away. Feeding her Pedialyte with an eyedropper, they drove straight to the hospital, where an IV was started immediately and she was admitted. The grandmother was given enough money to take care of her needs while she stayed with the child, and the Haiti Mission paid the hospital bill. On Saturday, when the surgery team met us at the airport to leave for home, they told us the little girl was alive and recovering.

Two paragraphs in the 1996 report point to an even wider effect of the Haiti Mission:

Through the efforts of the surgery team, two children (one an infant) in need of surgery for critical heart defects have been accepted at the Baptist Hospital in Winston Salem, North Carolina. They will be flown to the United States by team nurses as soon as possible, pending permission and visas from the U.S. government.

One of our interpreters was finally granted a visa, and he is now in Orlando, Florida, for surgery and therapy for his arm, damaged since birth. The help will be provided by one of our team doctors and her brother, an orthopedic surgeon.

Expanding in ever widening circles, the work of the surgeons continues. Only the future can judge the full impact of this vital part of the Haiti Mission.

CHAPTER 11

The Real Miracle

HOPEFULLY THE END OF THIS STORY WILL NOT BE WRITTEN UNTIL MANY YEARS INTO THE FUTURE. BUT AS THE TIME FOR its literary conclusion draws near, a few personal observations seem to be in order.

First, I acknowledge the presence of many miracles in this story. You have to be your own judge of that, but many of these events of the past twenty years seem to have little logical explanation. Nevertheless, as the events unfolded I became aware that these miraculous happenings were not the most important part of the story. Superseding any of these unusual occurrences is another miracle, which I view as the *real miracle*. Underlying everything else, it offers the only genuine hope for the future of the Haiti Mission.

In the beginning it seemed that this would be a tale of many miracles—a series of success stories occurring in one of the world's most forgotten places. It certainly began that way. The "boat" was a miraculous gift for a poor country and the delivery trip safe and successful beyond reasonable expectations. Even the later sale of the boat, with the appearance of a buyer as if by magic, was amazing. The well at Dondon was made possible by surprise surplus in a church budget, and the chance reading of a newspaper article. Time after time volunteers reported their lives were changed in Haiti, and prayers for help in trying times were often answered.

Mine is a very practical background, with little grounding in the miraculous. But as this story unfolded, an unseen presence and a guiding hand seemed to surround me. Yet, I also came face to face with failure. Obstacle followed obstacle; defeat followed close on the heels of other defeats. There were failures—far too many failures.

The Real Miracle

The fishing expeditions were a total failure. Why was there not a biblical miracle, nets full of fish, people fed, and hunger abolished? After a brief success the sewing project was abandoned; the irrigation project at Mazaire never really worked. Dream after dream never materialized. This story had its riots and roadblocks; plans put on hold and mission trips postponed. Pastors helped, but then moved on—their congregations feeling like victims of a typical Methodist disease, "Get a good preacher and the Conference takes him" syndrome.

For me, this presented a real dilemma. Should I gloss over the bad things and emphasize the good, stick to the miracles and ignore the rest? After all, one of the primary reasons for writing the story was to encourage new volunteers to come to Haiti. Since success often breeds success, it was tempting to highlight the successes and ignore the failures.

But this being a Christian mission the temptation was quickly set aside. Of course, it was good to have the consolation of knowing I was in good company. Although often called the "greatest book on earth," the Bible not only tells of miracles but is also full of stories of failures, of people with "feet of clay."

It was also good to remember that while the story of Jesus reports many miracles, Jesus did not use them to draw attention to himself or his ministry. To the contrary! After performing a miracle he often told the people, "Do not tell anyone." The legacy he wanted to leave behind was not his ability to perform miracles but his sacrificial offering of love.

Now, for whatever reason, the "story" took over, assuming its own direction. Turning away from the success of the mission, the focus shifted to the personal commitment and love of those who were a part of the Haiti Mission.

In his book *The Twain Shall Meet*, Dr. J. Harry Haines observed, "In some mysterious way the appalling need [in Haiti] seems to inspire people to attempt impossible tasks in the relief of human suffering, to give fresh hope to those who seem doomed to hopelessness and despair." This was the kind of commitment that consumed the Haiti volunteers and propelled their ministry of love. Even after many failures and defeats, they continued to come to Haiti, rarely completely successful but always faithful. A tribute to that kind of commitment is found in the report that this mission is "The longest continuous medical mission, in one place, by one church, in all of United Methodism."

The resolve of the Haiti Mission is well exemplified in the often-quoted creed of another group: "Neither snow, nor rain, nor heat, nor gloom of night stays these couriers from the swift completion of their appointed rounds" (U.S. Postal Service Creed).

Patients wait their turns expectantly to see doctors at the Tovar Clinic.

Even in the face of bleak and foreboding conditions, volunteers return year after year, doing what they can, for whomever they can. It is a commitment of love. And it is unconditional love. Like love between a husband and wife, it is "for better or for worse." Like a parent's love for a child, it does not love only when the child acts in the right way or seems to deserve it. It is love that continues in the best of times and the worst of times.

Bill White was asked, "Why do you keep going back to Haiti year after year?" He replied, "I don't know how to stop. This is what God asked me to do, and He hasn't changed His mind yet." Alice's response was similar, "Yes, I could *not* go. But I feel called to go, and I have to!"

With examples such as these, and many others like them, the real miracle (that should have been obvious in the beginning) becomes clear. The real miracle is a love that compels volunteers to share their love with brothers and sisters in Haiti—people often forgotten, sometimes undeserving, who don't always appreciate what is done in their behalf, but who are loved anyway. The real miracle is not in numbers healed or in missions accomplished. It is in the faithfulness of those who share their love in Haiti, for better or worse, in success or failure, taking on the form of a servant, and helping in a practical way.

Why do we always look for a different kind of miracle? Why does it take so long for us to recognize this kind? Living in a society that worships success, we usually measure it by some standard of winning, seldom in terms of service, and never in terms of failure. But we miss the point, forgetting that we profess to follow one who said, "Let him that is greatest among you, become like a servant."

We often forget that the gospel reverses the usually accepted standards of the world. Christ died on the Cross and became the supreme symbol of sacrificial love. Christians are never called to succeed but always called to be faithful to Christ—to the one who offered himself as a servant, was crucified, suffered, and died, but never ceased to love.

The Haiti Mission is now firmly forged in the shape of a cross. It is an offering of love in the name of Christ, frequently failing, sometimes suffering, often helping, but never ceasing. And it is love in the sense best described by St. Paul:

Love is patient;

Love is kind and envies no one.

Love is never boastful, nor conceited, nor rude; never selfish, not quick to take offence.

Love keeps no score of wrongs; does not gloat over other men's sins, but delights in the truth.

There is nothing love cannot face; there is no limit to its faith, its hope, and its endurance.

Love will never come to an end. (1 Cor. 13:4–8, *The New English Bible*; italics added for emphasis)

And therein lies the best hope for the future of the Haiti Mission. It is a miracle of sacrificial love, and *love never ends.*

CHAPTER 12

Does It Matter?

AS WE COME TO THE END OF OUR STORY, THERE IS A LINGERING QUESTION THAT DESERVES AN ANSWER. MANY people have been involved, and it is a fascinating tale, but does it matter? Is the Haiti Mission making any difference? Has it been worth the effort and time and money expended in its behalf over almost two decades? This is an honest question, and deserves an honest answer.

Betty Feezor, a member of Providence Church in its earlier years, once shared a motto by which she lived. It was framed in a needlepoint design she kept on her kitchen wall: "So live that when you are gone it will have mattered that you were here." This certainly expresses an almost universal wish that what we do will matter.

So, back to our question. What about the Haiti Mission of Providence United Methodist Church? Does it matter? Does this kind of volunteer service matter? Does all of this effort, infinitesimally small in the light of the human needs of the poorest nation in the world, make any difference?

Some would say no. Current statistics do not indicate that Haiti is any better off than it was in 1980. The hungry, the poor, and the sick are still there in overwhelming numbers. What does such a little bit of help offer in the face of such overwhelming need?

The cynics among us are even more negative. They often downplay efforts such as these, saying the volunteers are only going on glorified vacations in an "exotic" place. The money, they say, would be better spent in some form of direct aid.

So what do you think? What about this mission? A story, told and retold, bears repeating. Fishermen had been dragging their nets along the coast and piling up the catch along the beach. Other workers picked up the marketable fish and hauled them off in boxes. The very smallest fish were left littering the sandy beach.

A small boy, seeing the plight of the tiny fish floundering in the sand, began to pick them up, one by one, and toss them back into the ocean. A passerby watched for a while and then said to the boy, "You'll never get all the fish back, and it really doesn't matter anyway."

But as the boy threw the next one back he replied, "It matters to that one." That may be a make-believe story, but the examples from Haiti are real.

During one October mission trip, a father brought a limp, dehydrated, malnourished eight month old to the clinic. Maryse, the Haitian nurse, assisted by other clinic workers, spent the entire day administering penicillin and using an eye dropper, like feeding a baby bird, to feed Pedialyte orally to this child. Later it broke their hearts when the father gently picked him up to take him home. While he left with instructions and more of the solution for nourishment, the entire staff expected the infant to die.

The following February the same Haitian father appeared at the clinic, grinning from ear to ear, and presented his healthy, plump one year old whom "God had healed." It was the highlight of the trip. You could never convince one father, and an amazed group of medical volunteers, that what happened did not make a difference. "It mattered to that one," Louise Maybin said. Then recalling how the baby smiled and played, she added, "You can take care of one. One at a time is all you can do."

Louise and her husband Dr. Richard Maybin were realistic in their appraisal of what the medical teams could accomplish.

> We know that medically many were better from our visit, if only temporarily. Still, we realize that what the whole team did was only a *drop in the bucket*, but we remember what Jesus did with five loaves and two small fish. That gives us faith that our *drop* will make a difference. Each success is enough to keep us going.

On another occasion, a young boy named Michael looked up into the face of Dr. Maybin and said, "You're the only doctor I ever knew." Did that matter? You bet it did!

The individuals who have been helped matter. In addition, there is now hope that, with permanent clinics becoming available, the level of health of a whole region can be improved. It seems that the people appreciate very much having a community clinic, which they have never had before. For the most part they try to take good care of their children, and the clinic makes them feel as though they have access to medical help. They live in a world almost devoid of hope. But says Alice White, after a recent visit to the Tovar Clinic, "I can see hope now, in their faces. They

wait patiently for their turn, without complaint, dressed in their best."
As the report of 1997 activities at the Tovar Clinic pointed out:

> The clinic has been successful in its goal to bring a continuing health care program to the rural poor, thanks to a great many dedicated individuals who have provided funds and services, here and in Haiti. And with special thanks for the American team members who have become involved in this mission, going on faith to a place that was strange and formidable, committed to a cause they knew little about.

The report concluded with this affirmation: ". . . all who care about the Tovar Clinic, Haitian and American, patient and professional, will be ever grateful to God, for putting His hand on this effort."

The work of the medical teams from the Haiti Mission of Providence Church demonstrably has made a significant impact on one rural mountainous region in northern Haiti. But what about those who have gone to help? Did it matter to them? Speaking out of his experience, Bill White said, "If you go to Haiti you will never be the same again." Time and again this has been true.

Dee Brooks is a registered nurse, a wife, a mother of three children, an owner of two dogs and five cats, and a member of First United Methodist Church in Gastonia, North Carolina. In January of 1993 she went on what was to be the first of many journeys to Haiti. Follow along as she shares her story.

> I was invited to be part of a medical mission to Cap Haitien, sponsored by Providence United Methodist Church in Charlotte, and led by Alice and Bill White, members of that church. My home church in Gastonia provided the funds for me to be a part of that team.

> At this point in my life I had been a nurse for thirteen years, with primary experience in critical care nursing. I must say that the United States version of critical care and the Haiti version, while similar, are vastly different. Here there are all kinds of modern technology. In Haiti you use your critical care skills and ingenuity to provide care to very critically ill patients, without the auxiliary aid of machines or electricity. It is indeed a very eye opening and learning experience.

> With my preoccupation with my little world, I was woefully ignorant about conditions in other parts of the world. I am ashamed to say that with so many problems of our own in America, I felt we needed to take care of the poor and sick here before we tackled another country's poverty.

But all that changed when I held a Haitian child in my arms I thought was about two years of age, and discovered that she was actually seven. Or the infant, who had to be about four months old but was actually three years old.

It was then I realized that it didn't matter whether a child lived in Gaston County or in Haiti, God just wanted me to provide care for all his children. When I hold a Haitian child in my arms, I am truly aware that I am holding one of God's children in my heart! When you look into the eyes of the mother of the dying child in your arms, you know without a doubt there is nothing that separates the two of you, not miles, not cultures, not economy, nor religious beliefs. We are all one people, made by one God.

I pray that the opportunity to be part of this project is always available to me. I can't imagine what it would be like not to be able to return to Haiti to *hold his children.*

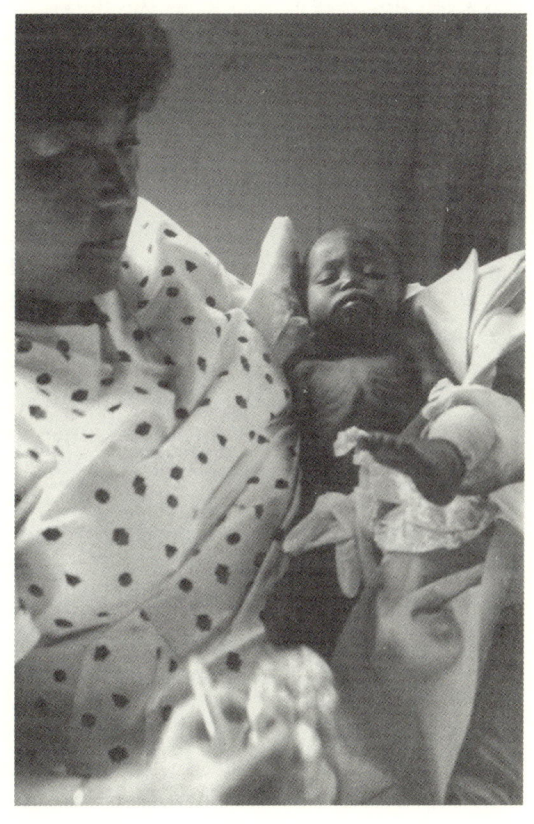

Dee Brooks holds a Haitian child.

Dee's experience has been repeated to some degree in almost every person who has been a part of this mission. Did being a part of a volunteer team matter? You bet it did! For almost every one of the volunteers, being a part of the Haiti Mission made a significant impact on his or her life.

The impact on Providence Church has mattered too. What began as an effort to single out a significant mission project in which members could have hands-on involvement in missions continues as the longest standing medical mission effort in the United Methodist Church by a single local church. Those who have participated are more deeply committed to their local church and continually inspire other members to become involved in some form of mission. The mission outreach of the church keeps expanding as more and more persons become personally aware that Christians not only hear the word but also *do it*.

Dr. Kennon L. Callahan, in *Twelve Keys to an Effective Church*, points out that one of the chief ways to evaluate an effective church is to see how well it measures up to his twelve "keys." The first key, and possibly the most important, is this: "A missional church has two or three specific, concrete, missional objectives." Specific means that it focuses on a particular human hurt and hope; concrete means that it delivers effective help; missional refers to helping individuals and institutions; and the objectives are to be clear enough for you to know when they have been achieved.

Dr. Callahan goes on to say:

> A church that shares an effective missional outreach with one or more human hurts and hopes becomes a legend on the community grapevine.... Much to its surprise ... it becomes a church that is more interested in helping than being helped. It becomes a church that is more interested in loving than being loved. It becomes a church that is more interested in giving than in getting. It becomes one of the distinctive churches in the community—a church that gives itself away in missional service.

The Haiti Mission has become a legend on a community grapevine that stretches across much of the United States. Does that matter to Providence United Methodist Church? I'm sure it does!

As the story ends, I can only conclude that the Haiti Mission does matter. And I am joined by hundreds who share in a resounding chorus of praise, "Yes, it has mattered!" It has mattered to Haitians; transformed the lives of many volunteers; heavily impacted the church which gave it birth and nurtured it across the years; and it has now become a beacon lighting the way and leading others into mission.

With that affirmation, we entrust the future of this mission into God's hands. But that still leaves a final question to be asked. Does it matter to *you*? What is it that God is calling you to do for the least of God's children where you live?

We have heard or read these words of Jesus, "Truly, I say to you, as you did it to one of the least of these my brethren, you did it to me" (Matt. 25:40 RSV). We may not all be called to go to Haiti or feel we should support this particular mission, but each of us is invited to do something.

We can become involved. We can help our church become involved. Each day, when we pray and give thanks for our blessings, we also can remember to pray for the least of God's children wherever they are. Most importantly, we can ask God to help us *do* something that will make a difference to them.

And there is a motto we should keep before us: "So live that when you are gone, it will have mattered that you were here."

APPENDICES

APPENDIX A
Chronology—Haiti Mission

APPENDIX B
Haiti Mission Directory (List of Participants)

APPENDIX C
Maps of Haiti

Appendix A

Chronology—Haiti Mission

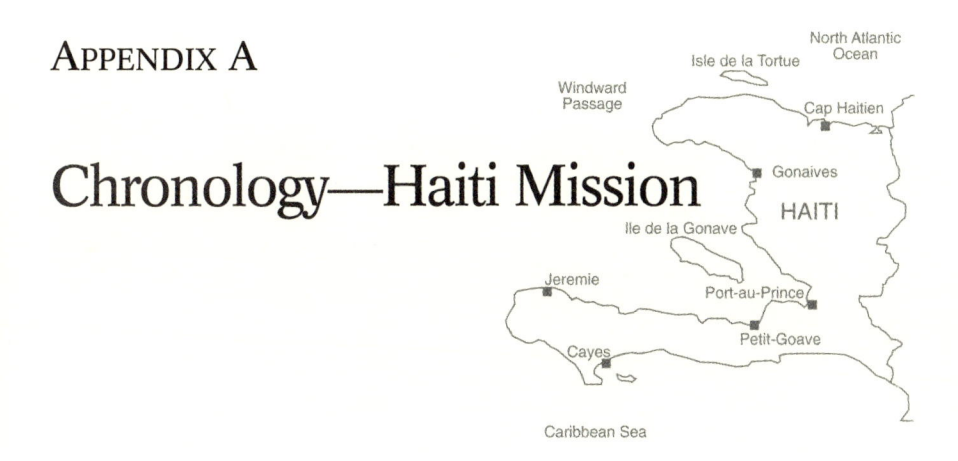

Providence United Methodist Church
Charlotte, North Carolina

1979   **Christmas Eve**
Bill White announces to his family gift of boat to the Methodist Church

1980   **February**
Boat accepted by Dr. J. Harry Haines, executive secretary of UMCOR
August 8–25
Pieces of Eight sails from Virginia to Haiti
December
Christmas Trip—recognition of Whites by Board of Directors of UMCOR

1981   **Summer**
Bill White to Haiti to work on the boat; Alice White begins nursing program

1982   **December 27 (1981)–January 3**
First fishing expedition
April 29–May 10
Second fishing expedition

The Real Miracle

1983   **December 27 (1982)–January 3**
"Look-See Mission"
December
Dondon well dug by Jack Hancox

1984   **June 28**
Pieces of Eight sold—80 percent of proceeds reserved for use at Dondon and Tovar Clinics

1985   **January 1–12**
First Haiti Mission team
Dr. Fred Miller—dental clinic in five towns
Roof trusses built and put in place at Dondon Clinic
January 16–26
Second Haiti Mission team
Dr. Walter Bullington—eye clinic in five towns
Roof at Dondon completed
Groundbreaking for Tovar Clinic
Summer
Rev. Ed Holmes leaves for England; Rev. Daniel Bartley appointed superintendent of Cap Haitien Circuit

1986   **December 30 (1985)–January 8**
Team I—dental clinics
Construction work at Tovar Clinic
Team II—canceled due to anti-government demonstrations against Jean-Claude Duvalier

1987   **January 9–18**
Dental clinics—Dr. Miller
Ophthalmology clinics—Dr. Bullington
First sewing clinic—Anne Bartley and Carolyn Boylan
Construction—completed major work at Tovar Clinic and secured roof structures at Tovar and Latannerie churches
Fall
Two wells dug at Mazaire by Jack Hancox and pumps installed in each

1988   **January 8–16**
Trip postponed due to violence associated with the January 1988 national elections

April 15–23
Medical clinics:
Ophthalmology—Dr. Bullington
Medical—Dr. Richard Maybin (first trip)
Dental—Dr. William James (first trip)
Sewing clinic—Bartley and Boylan
Construction—tables and cabinets built for Tovar Clinic; drip irrigation system installed at Mazaire

Summer
Rev. Gesner Paul replaces Rev. Bartley as superintendent of the Cap Haitien Circuit

1989 **January 13–21**
Medical teams to Tovar, Dondon, and Latannerie with M.D., ophthalmologist, dentist, and Dr. Ginnette Paul
Last sewing clinic—Ruth Royster
Construction—built pews and chancel furnishings for Dondon Church; completed interior floor at Tovar Clinic

October 13–28
Medical team with Dr. Maybin and Dr. Ginnette Paul to Tovar, Dondon, and Latannerie

1990 **January 12–18**
Ophthalmologist, M.D., and dentist at Tovar, Baudin, and Latannerie
Arrangements made with Hopital Le Bon Samaritain for 1991 surgical team
Construction—trusses built for new church at Champin and stored at Beck Hotel to await next team; floor and foundation completed by Haitian labor

October 20–26
Medical team with Dr. Maybin
Construction—erected trusses and completed roof at Champin with the help of six Haitian carpenters and other labor

1991 **January 17–25**
Trip postponed following civil disorder in Cap Haitien

February 15–23
Medical and dental team to clinics
Surgery (first surgery teams):

Dr. Walter Bullington at Baptist Eye Center in Cap Haitien
Dr. Mike Barringer at Hopital Le Bon Samaritain in Limbé
Construction—pews built for church at Champin; pilot, copilot, and mechanic of JAAR's aviation crew participate in construction

Palm Sunday
Opening service for Champin Church with over 300 present

1992

January 3–18
Trip postponed due to embargo imposed after overthrow of President Aristide in September of 1991

February
Bill and Alice White fly to Haiti with food and medicine

March 13–21
Medical team at clinics
Surgery at Baptist Eye Center and at Hopital Le Bon Samaritain
Construction—well at Latannerie repaired and money left to complete interior of sanctuary there

Summer
Rev. Lebrun Corsaire replaces Rev. Paul as superintendent of the Cap Haitien Circuit

October 16–24
Medical team at clinics
Surgical team at Hopital Le Bon Samaritain

1993

January 8–16
Medical team—two M.D.s and one dentist; 50 percent increase in number of patients seen
Eye surgery at Baptist Eye Center

January 8–23
Surgical team at Hopital Le Bon Samaritain

September 17–25
Medical team—two M.D.s at clinics
Surgical—one team at Hopital Le Bon Samaritain

1994

January 7–15
Medical team—two M.D.s and one dentist at clinics; Dr. Ernest Caesar, Haitian doctor worked with team

January 7–22
Surgical team at Hopital Le Bon Samaritain
November 8–15
Fall trip canceled because of U.S. invasion of Haiti and return of Aristide; Whites got special permission to fly to Haiti and, working with an all-Haitian team of doctors and nurses, saw 726 patients in five days

1995

January 4–12
Medical team—three M.D.s and one dentist
January 6–21
Two surgeons at Hopital Le Bon Samaritain
U.N. Police Moniteurs Internationale also barracked at the Beck Hotel
October 14–21
Medical team—nurses only on team—as a test worked entire week at Latannerie Clinic; saw almost 1,100 patients
October 20–28
Two surgeons at Hopital Le Bon Samaritain

1996

December 29 (1985)–January 15
Two teams back to back (12/29–1/6 and 1/5–1/14)
Largest group to date—five M.D.s, four surgeons, one periodontist, one anesthetist, six R.N.s, two medical technologists, and seven assistants
One week at Tovar, three days at Latannerie, and one day at Dondon; roadblock prevented team from going back last day of second week
1,874 patients seen in nine clinic days (350 by Haitian doctors the following week)
78 cases handled by surgeons in eight days
May 3–11
Roanoke, Virginia, United Methodist District medical team
A team of thirteen, including three M.D.s and one surgeon, one anesthetist, and eight nurses
Treated approximately 1,100 patients at Latannerie
Surgical team worked at Hopital Le Bon Samaritain
Summer
Rev. David Bidnell replaces Rev. Corsaire as superintendent of the Cap Haitien Circuit

October 11–19
Excess funding makes extra trip possible; thirteen team members including three M.D.s worked at Tovar Since Rev. Bidnell had just arrived from England, Bernard Gilles, Haitian interpreter, handled as many local arrangements for the trip as possible

1997

January 3–11
Medical team—three M.D.s and one periodontist; 1,000 patients seen at Tovar in five days
Surgical team—two surgeons at Hopital Le Bon Samaritain

January 10–18
Medical team—three M.D.s and one periodontist; 900 patients seen in four days at Latannerie; nationwide protest closed road last day
Surgical team—two surgeons at Hopital Le Bon Samaritain
Total surgical procedures for the two weeks—79

May
Roanoke, Virginia, medical team canceled by minister of health

May
Bill and Alice White go to Haiti and join Fiona Bidnell, Ichmide Morisset, director of development for the Cap Haitien Circuit, and Mme. Inette Durandis, directrice generale of programme from Port-au-Prince, and present a plan for licensing the Tovar Clinic to Dr. Jean Julien, the minister of health for the northern part of Haiti

May 20
Dr. Julien approves licensing of Tovar Clinic

September 23–30
Surgical team at Hopital Le Bon Samaritain

December
Tovar Clinic opened as full-time, fully staffed community health center

1998

January 9–17
Medical team—two M.D.s and one periodontist; first team to work with full-time Haitian staff at Tovar; health education team visits Latannerie Clinic

January 19–February 21
Surgical team—six surgeons at Hopital Le Bon Samaritain
May
Two M.D.s work with Haitian staff at Tovar
September/October
Surgical team—four surgeons at Hopital Le Bon Samaritain
October
Four M.D.s work with Haitian staff at Tovar

1999
January 8–16
Two M.D.s and one periodontist work with Haitian staff at Tovar
May 1–9
Three M.D.s work with Haitian staff at Tovar

Appendix B

Haiti Mission Directory

List of Participants (through May of 1999)

Mrs. Jodi Adams	Kings Mountain, North Carolina
Dr. David Armstrong	Roanoke, Virginia
Mrs. Ann Autrey	Charlotte, North Carolina
Mrs. Pearl Bacote	Kernersville, North Carolina
Mr. Royal Bacote Jr.	Kernersville, North Carolina
Dr. Michael Barringer	Shelby, North Carolina
Mr. Michael Barringer Jr.	Shelby, North Carolina
Mrs. Paula Barringer	Shelby, North Carolina
Ms. Julie Barringer	Shelby, North Carolina
Mrs. Sherry Basham	Roanoke, Virginia
Mrs. Carol Batman	Charlotte, North Carolina
Mrs. Kay Bearre	Huntersville, North Carolina
Mrs. Stephanie Berrier	Lexington, North Carolina
Mr. Paul Bonsall	Charlotte, North Carolina
Mrs. Jerre D. Boren	Elkin, North Carolina
Dr. Margarita Borrero	Longwood, Florida
Dr. Brooke Bostic	Charlottesville, Virginia
Mr. Doug Bowers**	Charlotte, North Carolina
Mrs. Betty Bowers	Charlotte, North Carolina
Mr. Alan Boylan	Charlotte, North Carolina
Mrs. Carolyn Boylan	Charlotte, North Carolina
Mr. Howard Boylan	Charlotte, North Carolina
Mr. Brian Brighton	Chapel Hill, North Carolina
Mrs. Dee Brooks	Gastonia, North Carolina

Mrs. Carol Brown	Charlotte, North Carolina
Mr. Eugene Brown	Charlotte, North Carolina
Mrs. Jean Broyles	Roanoke, Virginia
Dr. Walter Bullington**	Charlotte, North Carolina
Mrs. Shirley Bullington	Charlotte, North Carolina
Mr. Tom Burgess	Charlotte, North Carolina
Mrs. Dot Burns	Vale, North Carolina
Mrs. Annette Campbell	Ellenboro, North Carolina
Mr. Jim Cartwright	Waxhaw, North Carolina
Mrs. Mary Coleman	Charlotte, North Carolina
Mrs. Beverly Collins	Lincolnton, North Carolina
Ms. Marsha Clark	Lawndale, North Carolina
Mrs. Betty Cross	Matthews, North Carolina
Rev. Richard Daily	Forest City, Virginia
Mrs. Alicia Daily	Forest City, Virginia
Mr. John Davis	Charlotte, North Carolina
Mrs. Kathy Davis	Charlotte, North Carolina
Dr. Leigh Donowitz	Charlottesville, Virginia
Dr. David Duani	Earleysville, Virginia
Dr. James Detorre	Hilton Head, South Carolina
Sister Jacqueline Dewar	Rosman, North Carolina
Rev. Harley Dickson	Cornelius, North Carolina
Mrs. Inez Dickson	Cornelius, North Carolina
Ms. Sarah Dooley	Dalesville, Virginia
Dr. Joseph Duckwall	Roanoke, Virginia
Dr. Tom Fame	Salem, Virginia
Ms. Cyndi Favorite	Charlotte, North Carolina
Dr. Ray Ford	Charlottesville, Virginia
Mr. Rob Ford	North Garden, Virginia
Rev. George Freeman	Brevard, North Carolina
Mr. Roy Freeman	Charlotte, North Carolina
Dr. Virginia Gale	East Fallowfield, Pennsylvania
Mr. Jim Gale	East Fallowfield, Pennsylvania
Mr. Gerry Gardner	Waxhaw, North Carolina
Dr. Matthew Goldsmith	St. Louis, Missouri
Mrs. Mary Graham	Blowing Rock, North Carolina
Dr. Jayne Gunza	Huntersville, North Carolina
Dr. John Hanna	Rock Hill, South Carolina
Mr. Cory Hastings	Boone, North Carolina
Mr. Jim Hastings	Boone, North Carolina
Ms. Brenda Hawkins	Abingdon, Virginia
Mrs. Helen Henderson	Bloomingdale, Ohio
Mrs. Marty Henley	Charleston, West Virginia

Haiti Mission Directory   105

Mr. Grant Henley	Charleston, West Virginia
Ms. Jean Hogsed	Charlotte, North Carolina
Dr. William James	Matthews, North Carolina
Mrs. Myra Jenkins	Gastonia, North Carolina
Dr. Jack Johnson	Gainesville, Florida
Mrs. Ann Johnson	Gainesville, Florida
Ms. Jill Johnson	Matthews, North Carolina
Mr. Ed Johnson	Charlotte, North Carolina
Mrs. Dottie Johnson	Charlotte, North Carolina
Mr. John Jordan	Charlotte, North Carolina
Mrs. Susan Jordan	Charlotte, North Carolina
Dr. Sam Joyner	Greensboro, North Carolina
Ms. Brandi Kauth	Denver, North Carolina
Dr. Johnson Kelly	Shelby, North Carolina
Ms. Sandra Ketchie	Wadesboro, North Carolina
Mrs. Kelly Williams Kincannon	Columbia, South Carolina
Mrs. Kathy King	Charleston, West Virginia
Mr. Jack Kiser	Gastonia, North Carolina
Mrs. Melissa Kiser	Gastonia, North Carolina
Dr. Deysy Klein	Huntersville, North Carolina
Dr. Phillip Klim	Harrisonburg, Virginia
Mrs. Sydney Lancaster	Charlotte, North Carolina
Mr. Leo Lance	Waxhaw, North Carolina
Mrs. Anne Lance	Waxhaw, North Carolina
Ms. Suzanne LaPlace	Salem, Virginia
Dr. Robert Leadbetter	Charleston, West Virginia
Mrs. Ellie Leadbetter	Charleston, West Virginia
Ms. Caroline Leadbetter	Charleston, West Virginia
Mrs. Sara Masters	Charlotte, North Carolina
Dr. Richard Maybin**	Lawndale, North Carolina
Mrs. Louise Maybin	Lawndale, North Carolina
Ms. Heather McGarrah	Charlotte, North Carolina
Mr. Patrick Miller	Boone, North Carolina
Dr. Joe Minus	Shelby, North Carolina
Ms. Linda Mitchell	Durham, North Carolina
Ms. Lyda Moore	Ruskin, Florida
Mr. Don Monsees	Weaverville, North Carolina
Mr. Boyd McNeilly	Gastonia, North Carolina
Mrs. Cathy McNeilly	Gastonia, North Carolina
Dr. Fred Miller	Boone, North Carolina
Mrs. Susie Miller	Boone, North Carolina
Mr. Henry Moody	Newnan, Georgia
Dr. David Morris	Charlottesville, Virginia

Mrs. Mary Dee Parr	Charlotte, North Carolina
Mr. Wilton Parr	Charlotte, North Carolina
Ms. Cindy Payne	Marshville, North Carolina
Mr. Carl Poole	Lawndale, North Carolina
Mrs. Rose Poole	Lawndale, North Carolina
Dr. John Priddy	Roanoke, Virginia
Rev. Delores Queen	Salisbury, North Carolina
Mr. Tom Queen	Salisbury, North Carolina
Rev. Richard Randolph	Charlotte, North Carolina
Mrs. Wanda Randolph	Charlotte, North Carolina
Mrs. Vivian Richardson	Charlotte, North Carolina
Mrs. Katherine Robinson	Bessemer City, North Carolina
Mrs. Miriam Robinson	Vale, North Carolina
Mrs. Wanda Rogers	Shelby, North Carolina
Mrs. Gail Rogers	Asheville, North Carolina
Mr. Al Rose	Charlotte, North Carolina
Mrs. Helen Rose	Charlotte, North Carolina
Mrs. Ruth Royster	Cherryville, North Carolina
Dr. Kevin Rossiter	Columbia, Maryland
Mr. Raymond S. Rusak	Chatham, New Jersey
Captain Joe Sacchetti	Springfield, Pennsylvania
Ms. Terry Schoeps	Charlotte, North Carolina
Dr. Sam Stanford Jr.	Virginia Beach, Virginia
Ms. Sue Stephens	Charlotte, North Carolina
Mrs. Linda Love Talmadge	Charlotte, North Carolina
Dr. John Tenbrook	Perry Hall, Maryland
Mrs. Marian Thomas	Durham, North Carolina
Dr. Ben Timmons	Gastonia, North Carolina
Mr. Chen Vicente	San Juan, Puerto Rico
Mr. Richard Vinroot Jr.	Charlotte, North Carolina
Mrs. Sue Wertz	Roanoke, Virginia
Mr. Pete Weaver	Hilton Head, South Carolina
Mrs. Jean Weaver	Hilton Head, South Carolina
Mrs. Alice White	Gloucester, Virginia
Mr. A. R. (Bill) White	Gloucester, Virginia
Rev. Larry Wilkinson	Lake Junaluska, North Carolina
Dr. Larry Whitten	Harrisonburg, Virginia
Mrs. Novelyn Williams	Gastonia, North Carolina
Mr. Andrew Wolff	St. Louis, Missouri
Dr. Patricia Wolff	St. Louis, Missouri
Mrs. Connie Whaley	Reston, Virginia
Mrs. Jane Williams	Cedar Mountain, North Carolina
Mr. John Young	Shelby, North Carolina

** Deceased

Appendix C

Maps of Haiti

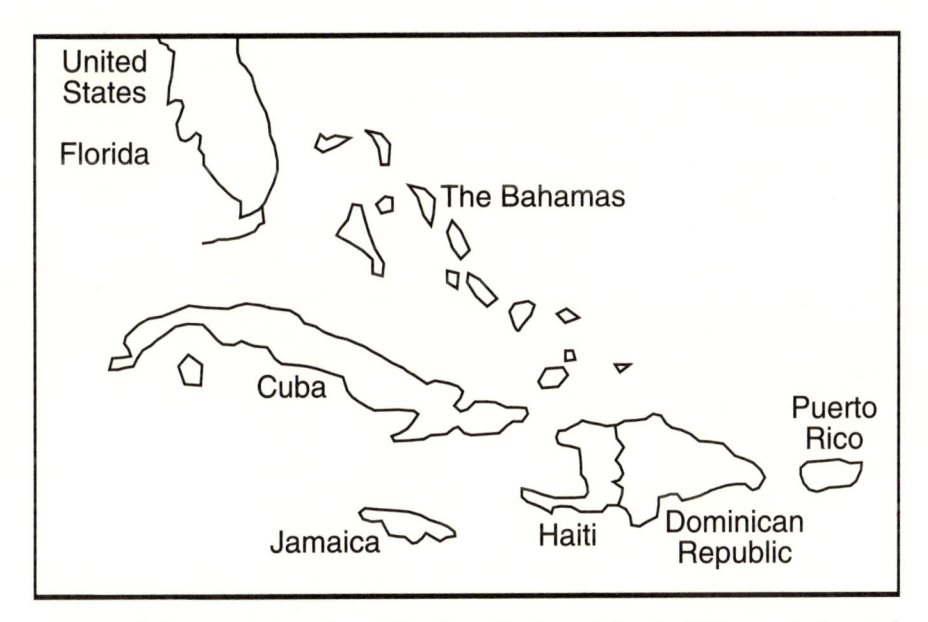

Haiti and the Dominican Republic share the large island of Hispanola located between Cuba and Jamaica to the west, and Puerto Rico to the east.

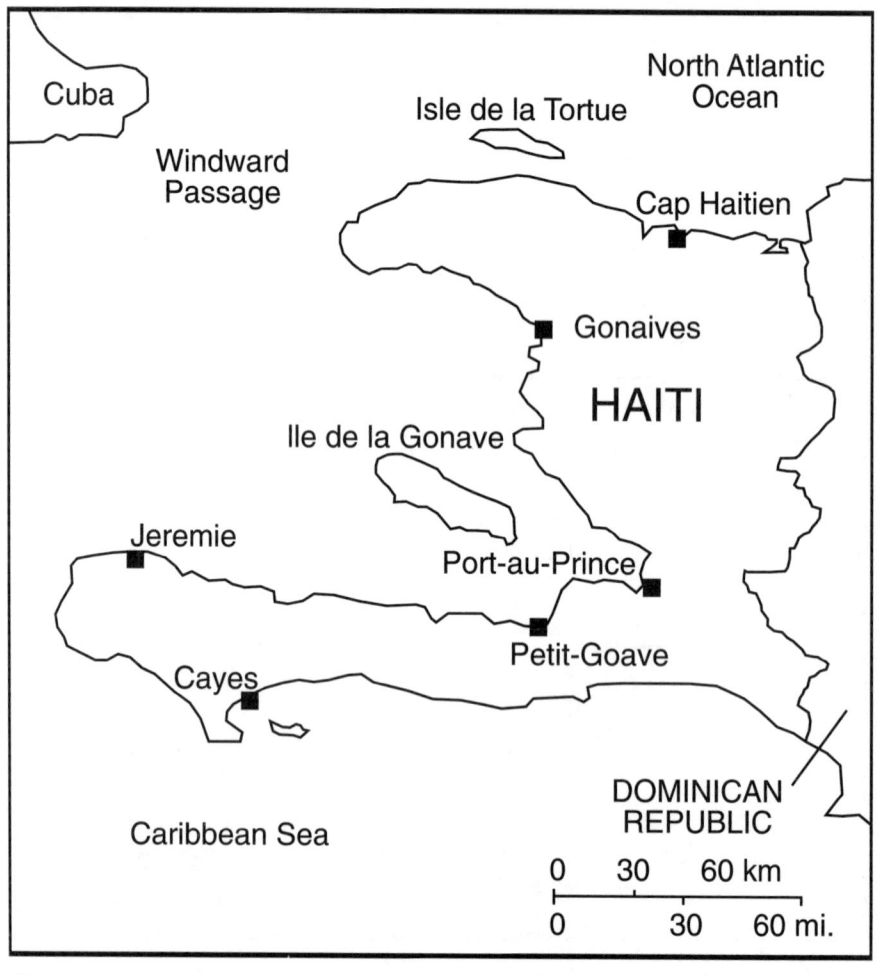

The nation of Haiti, with its principal towns and cities.

Maps of Haiti 109

CAP HAITIEN AREA

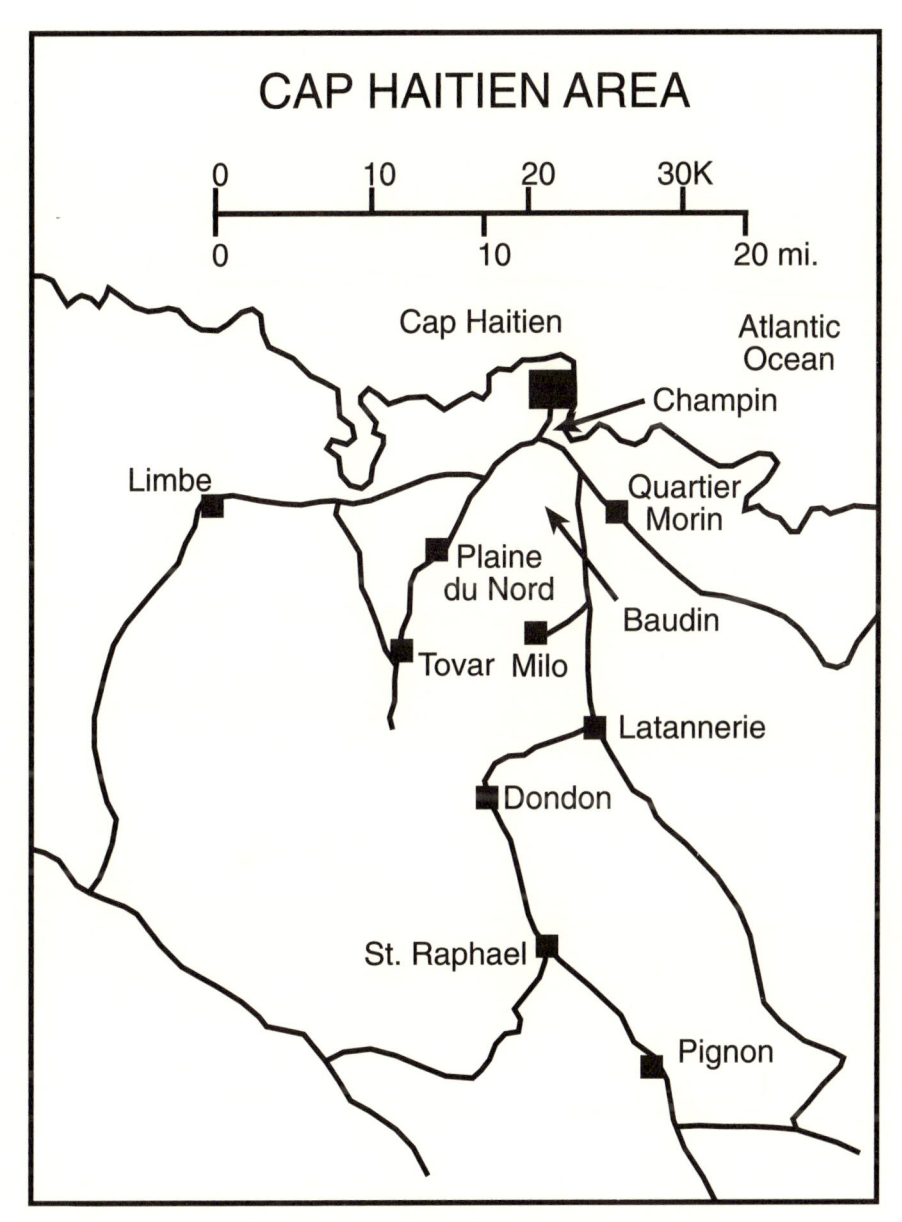

The Cap Haitien area in the northern part of Haiti, showing the location of churches and towns referred to in The Real Miracle.

Index

Abraham, Sadrac, 78
Aldersgate United Methodist Church, 74
American Baptist Convention, 75, 80
Angus, Jean, 25
Aristide, President, 64, 68
Autrey, Ann, 60–61
Baptist Eye Center, 64, 75–76
Baptist Hospital, 81
Baptist Mission, 26, 74
Baptist Mission Board, 31
Barringer, Michael L., 6, *50-4*, *50-8*, 64, 74–80, **77**
Bartley, Anne, *50-7*, 57–58
Bartley, Daniel, *50-7*, 53–54, 56–58, **57**, 63
Baudin, Haiti, 51, 54, 59, 67
Beck, Kurt, 40
Beck Hotel, 40, **40**, 45, 54, 59, 69
Bidnell, David, 71–73
Bidnell, Fiona, 72–73
Board of Global Ministries. *See* General Board of Global Ministries
Boggan, Bob, 58
Bonsall, Paul, **52**, 53
Boren, Mrs. Jerre, 71
Borrerro, Margie, **76**
Bowers, Betty, 48, *50-8*
Bowers, Doug, 35, 46, *50-8*

Boylan, Carolyn, 24, 46, *50-7*, *50-8*, 57–58
Boylan, Howard, 24, 33, 35, 41, 46, *50-8*, **53**
Bradley, Kenneth, Jr., **20**, 22
British Methodist Church, 26
Brooks, Dee, 70, 88, **89**
Brown, Carol, 45, 47–48, 61
Broyles, Jean, 70
Bullington, Shirley, **47**, 48, *50-8*, 55, 61, 64, 75–76, **77**
Bullington, Walter G., 44, 48–49, *50-5*, *50-8*, 55, 61–62, 64, 74–75
Burmeister, John, 11
Callahan, Kennon L., 90
Cannon, Hillary, 54
Cap Haitien, Haiti, 6, 27, 30, 39–41, 45, 49–50, *50-7*, 52, 55–56, 58, 63–66, 68, 72, 74–75, 88
Cap Haitien Church, *50-7*
Cap Haitien Circuit, 27–28, 33, 45, 51–54, 59, 64, 66, 71–73
Carolinas Medical Center (Charlotte, N. C.), 79
Cartwright, Jim, *50-8*
Cato, Gaetane, 14
Central Piedmont Community College (Charlotte, N. C.), 18

Champin, Haiti, *50-5*, *50-6*, 51, 58–59
Champin Church, 59
Charlotte District Mission Society, 21
Charlotte Observer, 12
Christian Institute for Rural Life, 26
Citadelle, 50
Clark, Hollis, 64, 74–75
Clark, Marsha, 71
Cleveland Memorial Hospital (Shelby, N. C.), 79
Clymer, Wayne K., 17
Coconut Villa Hotel, 40, 44
Coleman, Mary, 4, **65**
College Bird Church, 26
Congregational Development and Church Growth for the Texas Conference, 54
Coordination of Development (COD), 72
Corsaire, Lebrun, 66–67, 70
Corsaire, Margaret, 67
Costeau, Jacques, 23
Cotswold Elementary School, 33
Daily, Alicia (White), 9–11
Daily, Dick, 9–11, 24, **30**
Depestre, Marco, 26, 50
Detorre, James, 75
Dickson, Harley, 24
Dickson, Inez, 24, 46, 49, *50-8*
Dieveaux, Giovennes, 20, **20**
Domond, Edouard, 16, 22, 34–35, 54
Dondon, Haiti, 6, 27, 29–36, **32**, 38–39, 41, 44–46, **46–47**, 48, *50-6*, 51–52, 54, 58–59, 66, 70, 82
Dondon Clinic, 42, 44
Duke University Divinity School, 10
Durandis, Mme. Inette, 72
Dussex, Alberto, 18, *50-2*
Duvalier, Jean-Claude ("Baby Doc"), 54–55
Eastern Airlines, 39, 55
Edy (the interpreter), 47–48, 61
Eglisé Methodiste d'Haiti. *See* Haitian Methodist Church
Fadley, Tommy, 10
Fadley, Vera, 10
Feezor, Betty, 86

First United Methodist Church (Gastonia, N. C.), 88
Ford, Raymond, 73
Freeman, George, 5, *50-7*
Fréres, Haiti, 24
Gale, Ginny (White), 11, *50-3*, 78
Gardner, Gerry, *50-8*
Gary, Kays, 12
General Board of Global Ministries, 21, 28
Gilles, Bernard, 71
Goldsmith, Matthew, 71
Gonaives, Haiti, 54
Goodhand, Jeanette, 43
Grace Children's Hospital, 50
Guido, 15
Haines, Harry, 10–11, 15-16, **16**, 22, 83
Haitian Methodist Church (Eglisé Methodiste d'Haiti), 5–6, 15, **16**, 20, 22, 26–28, 33–35, 38, 41–42, 50–51, 54–55, 58, 62, 67, 70
Haitian Ministry of Health, 6, 42
Haiti Mission Committee, 35, 38
Hancox, Donna, 31
Hancox, Jack, 31
Handbook for United Methodist Volunteers in Mission, The, 60
Heinl, Nancy, 25
Heinl, Robert, 25
Henderson, Helen, 57
Henley, Steve, 55, 61
Highland Park United Methodist Church, 10
Hodges, Emily, 80
Hodges, Joanna, 78
Hodges, William H., 63–64, 75, **76**, 80
Hogsed, Jean, 61
Holley, Sister Paulette, 25
Holmes, Ed, 27–29, **30**, 33–34, 36, 42, 44–46, 53–54, 72
Hopital Le Bon Samaritain (Hospital Good Samaritan), 6, *50-3*, *50-4*, 64, 67, 70, 75, **76–77**, 78–80
Hopital Le Bon Samaritain (HBS) Foundation, 80
Internal Revenue Service, 39
Isidore, Maryse, 64, 87

Index

JAARS, 56
James, Bill, 4, *50-4*, 61
Jeremie, Haiti, 15, 27
Johnson, Dottie, 24
Johnson, Ed, 24–25
Jordan, John, 45
Jordan, Susan, 45, **53**
Joyner, Sam, 70
Julien, Jean Myrtho, 72
Kelly, John, 78
Klein, Deysey, 78
Klim, Philip, 78
Lacy, Elizabeth, 11
Lacy, Hank, 11
La Gonave, Haiti, 15
Lamb, Cliff, 36, 54
Lance, Leo, *50-8*
Latannerie, Haiti, 6–7, 27, 42, 51–52, 54, 56, 59, 65–67, 70–71, 73
Latannerie Clinic, *50-5*, **65**, 69
Lay Training Center, 24
Ledbetter, Robert, 78
Limbé, Haiti, 6, 63–64, 67, 74–76, 81
Lions Club, 48
Love, William, 11
Love, Mrs. William, 11
Luke (carpenter), *50-5*
Lynx International, 56
Martin, Charlie, *50-6*
Maybin, Louise, *50-8*, 62, **63**, 87
Maybin, Richard, *50-8*, 62, **62**, 66, 71, 77, 87
Mazaire, Haiti, 51, 56, **57**, 83
Methodist Churches of the Caribbean and the Americas (MCCA), **16**, 33
Methodist Clinic of LaSaline, 25
Methodist Publishing House, 9
Michael (young patient), 87
Miller, Fred, 44–45, 47–48, 61–62
Miller, Susie, 47–48, 61
Minnick, Katie, 78
Minus, Joe, 67
Mission Aviation Fellowship, 55
Mission Flights International (MFI), 68
Mitchell, Linda, *50-8*
Morisset, Ichmide, 72

Morrison Church (Leesburg, Fla.), 9
Morton, Paul, 22, 34
Neal, Benny, 19–20, **20**, 22, 24–25, **26**, 27, 35, *50-2*
Neal, K. D., 19–20
Neal, Kevin, 19–20
Neal, Linda, 19, 22
OAS, 64
Parr, Mary Dee, 46, **47**, *50-8*
Parr, Wilton, 46, **47**, *50-8*
Paul, Gesner, *50-5*, *50-8*, 58, 64–66, 71
Paul, Ginnette, 64, 66, 71
Petit Goave, Haiti, 26
Petit Goave Circuit, 58
Pettinger, Betty, 31
Pieces of Eight, 8–15, **13**, **16**, 18–19, **20**, 26, 35, *50-1*, 78
Pike, Don, 54
Plain du Nord, 46, 51, 53
Poole, Carl, 64, 77
Port-au-Prince, Haiti, 10, 13–15, 17, 24–25, 27–28, 31, 35–36, 39–41, 44, 50, *50-1*, 54–55, 72, 77
Port-au-Prince Methodist Church, 25, 35
Providence Outreach Commission, 33, 35
Quartier Morin, 47, 51
Randolph, Richard, *50-8*
Randolph, Wanda, *50-8*
Red Cross, 33
Richmond Times-Dispatch, 31
Roanoke Lion's Eyeglass Recycling Center, 71
Robinson, Leroy, 30
Rogers, Gail, 71
Rogers, Wanda, *50-8*, 76, **77**
Rose, Al, 21, 24, 27, 29–33, 35–36, 41, 45, 47, **53**
Rose, Helen, 24–25
Rossiter, Kevin, 71
Royal Haitian Hotel, 18
Scrivener, Ray, 11, 14
Selph, Charles, 54
Shepherds Center, 33
SS *Manley Rodgers*, 8
Stephens, Sue, *50-8*, 76, **77**

St. Paul, 85
Thomas, Marian, **65**
Timmons, Ben, 78
Tovar, Haiti, 3, 7, 27, 33–34, 36, 39, 41–42, 47, *50-3*, *50-6*, 51, 53–54, 56, 59, **63**, 65–66, 70–71, 75, 80–81
Tovar Clinic, 6–7, 38, 44, *50-2*, **52–53**, 56, 58, 61, 72–73, **84**, 87–88
Twain Shall Meet, The, 83
Twelve Keys to an Effective Church, 90
UN (United Nations), 68
UNICEF, 31
U.N. International Police Monitors, 69
United Methodist Church, 22, 41, 43, 90
United Methodist Committee on Relief (UMCOR), 10–11, 17, 19–20, 22, 28, 34, 51, 55
  Board of Directors, 17
  Finance Committee, 30–31
  Specialized Ministries, 34
United Methodist Volunteers in Mission (UMVIM), 19
University of Manchester (U.K.), 72
U.S. Treasury Department, 68
Volel, Mr., 36
Western North Carolina (WNC) Conference of the United Methodist Church, 28, *50-6*, 58–59

White (family), 8, 50
White, Alice, 6–7, 9, 11–12, 16–18, 20, **20**, 22–24, 28, 40, 42, 48, 50, *50-2*, *50-3*, *50-5*, *50-8*, 55–56, 60–61, 65–70, 72–73, 75–78, **76**, 87–88
White, A. R., Sr., 9
White, Bill (A. R. Jr.), 7–12, **13**, 15–24, **16**, **21**, 27, 29, **30**, 31, 34–37, 40, 42, 46, *50-5*, *50-8*, **52**, 53–56, **57**, 59, 61, 65, 68, 70, 72–73, 76–78, 81, 84, 88
White, Ginny. *See* Ginny White Gale
White, Paul, 11, 19
White, R. M., Jr., 11
White, R. M., Sr., 11
White, Rob, 11, 18
White, Mrs. Rob (Kathy), 11
White and Co., 39
Whitten, Larry, 78
Wilkinson, Larry, 37, 45, *50-6*, 54–55, 58, 62
Williams, Kathy, 45
Williamson, E. H., 11
Willow Creek Community Church, 75
Wolff, Patricia, *50-6*
World Health Organization (WHO), 72
Written in Blood, 25